A BOUQUET of POEMS

Dr. Pulak Sahay

INDIA · SINGAPORE · MALAYSIA

A BOUQUET of POEMS

Dr. Pulak Sahay

notionpress.com

INDIA • SINGAPORE • MALAYSIA

ISBN
Paperback 979-8-89556-045-7
Hardcase 979-8-89588-693-9

Contents

Foreword

It is becoming increasingly common for medical practitioners and researchers to write novels or works of that genre to analyse and explicate the nature and consequences of human illnesses and ailments. This has not yet extended to plays or poetry, largely because these literary mediums do not yield so easily to the articulation of issues the writers intend to write about. This difficult medium of poetry is what the author of this book has attempted to tackle.

This book is a collection of poems on diverse subjects written over a period of eighteen years and encompassing such subjects as nature, emotions, philosophy, political scenarios, places, festivals, current global events, family connections, abstract thoughts and the author's own state of being. There are sixty-three poems in this anthology.

Through these poems the author tries to look for the underlying meaning of life, and seek the truth in its various aspects. Poetry has become a mechanism, in his practice of medicine in general and gastroenterology in particular, which keeps him focussed on his goal of spreading education among the general public regarding Reflux disease, including its day-to-day management, significant complications, poor quality of life, and life threatening complications like cancer of the food pipe, the fastest growing cancer in the West, and also rising in India.

The purpose of the book is to generate revenue by the sale of the book, which will go to CARD (Campaign Against Reflux Disease), a registered UK-based charity whose sole purpose is to promote the fight against reflux globally, but predominantly in UK and India. The purpose could also have been realised in other ways, but the poetic form was chosen in the hope that it will enhance literary sensibility in the masses, and cultivate a love of poetry.

One might ask why the author should be concerned about the risk of reflux. He could leave it alone and tackle its consequences. Why should he spend his time, energy, and money spreading this advice? The answer obviously is his sense of responsibility, as the level of knowledge of the disease is poor. The doctor is not only concerned with the cure, but also with the prevention of reflux. This introduces a new ethical element in the discussion, namely, redefining the purpose of the medical discipline. But once we recognise this, we have to conclude that not just a particular branch of medicine but the entire discipline should have this aim and concentrate on preserving health, rather than tackling ill-health. Once this becomes accepted as the main objective of medical training, our whole approach changes and the kind of charity that the author is talking about becomes an integral part of the medical profession. Surely a laudable aim.

The author of this collection of poems is a distinguished gastroenterologist, professionally well-known, and also respected for his public concern. The book deserves to be read and reflected upon.

Bhikhu Parekh

August 2024

Lord Bhikhu Parekh is a Fellow of the British Academy and a Centennial Professor at the London School of Economics, a Visiting Professor at Harvard University and at the University of Pennsylvania and Emeritus Professor at University of Hull. Formerly a Vice-Chancellor at the University of Baroda, he is the recipient of the Padma Bhushan from Government of India. He was awarded the BBC's Lifetime Achievement Award and is a Freeman of the City of Hull.

Preface

Reflux is ubiquitous. It hurts, but still patients don't treat it with respect. They feel that reflux is part of life and nothing to complain about. They least realise that the complications of reflux can be devastating, akin to the iceberg, looking innocuous but deadly, drifting towards the Titanic. To begin with, the quality of life can be vitiated by Reflux, while at the other extreme it can lead to oesophageal cancer which is the fastest growing cancer in USA and is making its presence felt in Asia as well.

This fills me with trepidation & frustration, and the best way I can cope with it, is by writing poetry. In this mad and senseless world, this is what helps me keep my sanity. This creative pursuit is something that I have now indulged in, for nearly two decades. And the culmination of my efforts is *"A Bouquet of Poems"*.

It has been triggered by the miracle of nature and life, frolicking all around me, and the myriads of emotions that have caressed my inner being. But then when I see the thousands of people with reflux, suffering in silence, my heart burns. I want to go on to the rooftops and shout myself hoarse like Demosthenes, trying to tell everyone to take heed. Or if I had the help of Shakespeare, then I would become an Antony, who could ruffle up the spirits and put a tongue in every patient, that would make the very stones of London, New York and Delhi to rise up and take notice. But this like Hamlet's situation, is not to be!

And hence I resort to circulating the message of "CARD" tangentially, by promoting it through my book of poetry. A book that delves into all aspects of life's emotions, nature, politics, family and philosophy. It also opens a window into my own soul and I can see myself with all my frailties which reflect and portray the multiple facets of my patients, as embodied by the common man. So I feel that even if one man reads *"A Bouquet of Poems"* and is affected positively by the poems therein, then it would be the first step in the journey of a thousand miles.

Dr. Pulak Sahay
Wakefield, UK
23rd May 2024

Inspired by my mother Dr. Usha Sahay, whose ethos in life was spreading love and succour to one and all without expectation, I take a leaf out of her life and dedicate this creation of mine to the millions of patients of Reflux Disease all over the world and hope that my effort in launching *"A Bouquet of Poems"* will bring some joy to them, and go a long way in alleviating their plight.

Dedication

Dr. Usha Sahay
Retd. Professor & Head of Dept. Obs. & Gynae
RIMS, Ranchi, Jharkhand, India

To begin with, I need to express my gratitude to my family of poets, called *"Suniye-Sunaiye."* This group, of which I am a founder member is a choir of poets, based in Yorkshire, UK.
We stimulate each other to write, and then congregate every few months, to listen to each other's poetry. This has stimulated me to no end, and has led me to write, on a regular basis.

Then there is my own *family*, who have helped me, by giving me full liberty. They have never interfered with my poetic pursuits, and have given me ample space, and leeway to create my poetry.

My late mother, however, was a different kettle of fish. She was my ardent fan, and looked for every opportunity to listen to my poems, appreciated them and encouraged me to write more. This book, therefore, is dedicated to her.

Acknowledgements

Now in the typical Shakespearean flourish, last but not least, I need to thank my friend and brother, *Amit Shahi*, without whose help and support, this anthology of poems would not have seen the light of day.

It is through him that I have had the good fortune of getting *Divyangani Sharma*, working on my project. It is she who has taken the individual poems and with her artistry and dexterity arranged them, into an exquisite bouquet. To her go my heartfelt thanks.

And finally there is the *reader*, the ultimate judge and arbiter. If the reader says "Yeah" then my goal is achieved, as I have, as always worked, on this compendium of poems, with the aim that the CARD Charity gets the entire proceeds of all the sales of my book.

Dr. Pulak Sahay
Wakefield, UK

The wind does whistle
And the leaves rustle,

The humming bees do the flowers tease.
The swoop of the eagle over splashing waves,
Frolicking dolphins do the fish chase.
Unfolding of the daffodil announces the Spring,

Patter of the raindrops
Follow the crackle of lightning.
The chirping of the birds
accompanies the dance of the peacocks,

The song of the cricket
Is interrupted by the woodpecker's knocks,

The butterflies flit
flapping their wings,

Dawn ascends
and the cuckoo sings.

Nature's orchestra is
playing its symphony.

The music is melodious
and in perfect harmony.

Nature's Symphony

Why am I so empty? Why am I so sad?
The sun is shining,
The weather is bright.
The flowers are in full bloom,
The birds are in flight.
Why do I feel so empty? Why do I feel so sad?
A gentle breeze is blowing,
The squirrels play with content.
The trees sway in the wind,
With a musical intent.
Why am I so empty? Why am I so sad?
The stars are out,
With the moon at night.
The fireflies dance,
With abandon and delight.
Why do I feel so empty? Why do I feel so sad?
My love has deserted me,
Which earlier was mine.
She said she would always love me,
But now she has no time.
There are other more important things that occupy her life,
So the emotional deprivation has caused this internal strife.

All the promises of always loving and never leaving me have gone in vain,
I had heard and believed that once, true love-it would always remain,
But I think these probably are empty words, which are there to give you pain.
I am now hurt, I am forlorn, I am lost,
For I love her so much that I couldn't care for the cost.
Now that I don't have my love beside me,
Holding my hand, giving me support and always thinking of me.
In spirit telling me that she would always be there, especially when times were bad,
That is why I feel so lonely, so desolate, so sad!

Sadness

A smile that blossoms on your lips when your toddler takes his first step
                Akin to you as the soaring flight of a dove
A twinkle appearing in your eyes when you hear the crystal laughter of your lady love.
Lyrics escaping your soul at four decades and twenty,
                When you listen to the melody from the swinging sixty.
Spontaneously tapping your feet as the rock band plays your favourite number
The effort of your child at sports day, the exhaustion,
                but following his win, he lost in peaceful slumber.
Dancing wet in the first monsoon showers,
                For your lover's birthday making a bouquet of flowers.
Listening to the chirping of birds welcoming the dawn,
                Watching the deer nudging, caring and licking her newborn fawn.
Crimson skies painted with gay abandon by the sun,
Cool breeze enthusing the children to go out in the park and have some fun.
Sitting beneath the night sky watching the stars and the moon,
                Lovers holding hands, gazing into each other's eyes, humming a tune.
Rainbow coloured butterflies adding a splash of colour to spring,
                Squirrels collecting nuts and over treetops frolicking.
Happiness is the little things in life which count a lot,
Something that money can't buy and where power and influence always fall short.

Happiness

Thinking of you, when apart
Thinking of you, as you are close to the heart.

The vision of angelic beauty and doe eyes with kohl,
Pools of blue lagoon, through which you can peer into the
soul.

Tinkling laughter, pouring out of the heart
Glow of smile never abates, once it starts.

Slim waist, inviting an embrace
Swaying walk, so full of grace.

Shapely ankles complement the seductive hips
Rouge cheeks blossom into full lips.

Slender fingers, have the magical touch,
Musical voice, encompasses one in its clutch.

The phone is on vibrate, calls missed while driving,
The ring on divert, phone not answered when in a meeting.

Inspite of that I still miss you,
Because it is you - I think of you.

Thinking of You

It starts with birth - the advent of the child,
The anticipation and then the child's arrival drive the parents wild.
House gets rearranged and there are toys galore,
Life revolves around the baby and no task is a chore.
The relatives leave and friends have gone home,
Your husband is out at work and you have nowhere to roam.
Day in and day out, the novelty is wearing thin,
No respite from work and soon there is no joy within.
Then many moons later he is a school-going lad,
You revel in his success and for his achievements you are glad.
The boy, now a handsome man, has found a girl,
Soon he leaves home after a whirlwind swirl.
House is once again empty - there is just the two of you,
You sit in front of the TV as there is nothing to do.
Making a career was once life's sole aim,
Happiness is not automatic by achieving local acclaim.
Appreciation at work and promotion are a means to an end,
Self-satisfaction is the key on which happiness does depend.
Acquaintances come and go - they should not make an impact,
Being successful at business at all costs can from life distract.

Life is short and is for living to the full,
Success and money are important but enjoying it with your love
is really wonderful.
Forget the heartache and the pangs of despair,
Remember the smiles, the gifts and the good times you got to share.
Sitting in a café, drinking coffee, holding each other's hands,
Talking animatedly, joking and just being together feels grand.
Trough follows peak and life does ebb and flow,
But do remember that after a dark thundery shower the sky gets adorned
by a rainbow.

Peaks and Troughs

Pulak Sahay

How high is the Everest
How deep is the ocean
What about the tsunami's crest
And the atom's perpetual motion.

How much colour in the rainbow
How much fragrance in the flowers,
How one gets respite from the heat
By the monsoon showers.

What about the sand grains in the desert
And ice in the polar caps,
How many stars in the skies
And all the people in the world map.

How much shine in the sun
How much wind in hurricane,
What is the expanse of space
And the shape of rain.

How hot is a raging fire
How cool is the moon,
How soothing is the music played in tune.

How much do I love you
I don't know,
More than you
I would say so.

How Much Do I Love You

Why is the sky so blue?
Why is God called true?
How did Everest rise so high?
What makes the migrating birds fly straight through the sky?
Why does the sun rise in the east?
Why do people enjoy a feast?
Where does the hurricane get its power?
Why is it soothing to get wet in the monsoon shower?
Why do the salmon go upstream to spawn?
How many millions are there in the great sardine run?
From where do the blue whales appear at dawn?
Why do iguanas eat algae from the bottom of the ocean?
Why is the rose red?
Why is the grass green?
Why does X-ray not pass through lead?
Why does England have a queen?
Why does it hurt to love?
What is so pure about a white dove?
Why is jealousy so vile?
Why does a blushing bride look so fragile?
Why did the human race occur?
After death where do we land?
All these questions have no answer.

Hence life and Nature are so difficult to understand.
So forget these imponderable questions and live life in the present,
Love and help everyone and never torment.
Forget what will happen tomorrow,
If today is taken care of then there will be no sorrow.
Heaven and Hell are here on earth,
It is all a state of the mind.
Dealing with life is not a matter of mirth,
But it can be done, if the heart is pure and kind.

The forest canopy has a greenish hue,
In the morn the green grass is laden with dew.
The plants in the garden show off their green leaves,
The leap of the green grasshopper is beyond belief.
The green of the deep sea beckons the turtle,
Towards the dark green of the sardine school, the dolphins hurtle.
The green algae of the Galapagos does the iguana entice,
Holding their breath underwater is difficult,
But for this green delight, they are willing to pay the price.
Witnessing peoples' success even friends can occasionally turn green,
Leading to one of the deadly sins with comrades turning mean.
The first time parliamentarians are also usually green,
Time seasons them and then they learn to skim the cream.
Lovers like to hold on to memories keeping them green,
Nostalgia soars like an elegant swan.
Never letting the shine come off the sheen,
Remembering the past like yesterday's dawn.
Then there is the green of precious emerald,
When around the neck of Juliet a sparkle it does herald.
Catching the eye of Romeo who then has no control,
Falling hopelessly in love and in the process losing his soul.

Green is an integral part of the rainbow,
Without it the heavens' painting would be a poor show.
The skies would be dull, drab and grey,
Indicating that the Gods in their abode had lost their spark and sway.
The green cape of the Amazon welcomes the warm showers,
The greenish depth of the ocean instills an unbelievable calm.
The green carpet of many a garden encourages the bees to visit the flowers,
The green crest of mountaintops exudes majesty and charm.
Green is the universal colour,
The current mantra of being "green" reigns supreme.
Green attitude is what will bring to all the much needed succour,
In this global turmoil "green" encouraging paradise lost
to be regained, should be mankind's ultimate dream.

The Colour Green

The tree is on fire with leaves orange, red and bright,
Winds ruffle it up and there is a reddish orange carpet in sight.
The canopy of trees is now no longer around
Its proud crest sweeps the ground.
Barren trees stand forlorn and dejected,
They were one with Nature but now seem rejected.

Dark days with long nights gets to be oppressing,
Waiting for light and not getting it is depressing
But before light there will be cold,
First silvery winter and then summery gold.

The birds lazily wake up,
The haze does rise.
Wintry dawn crackles,
Sunbeams skate on ice.

Icicles drip from conifers,
Snowflakes brush lovers cheeks.
The pristine white beckons,
Waterfalls are frozen in the creeks.

Frost thaws and the filmy gossamer disappears,
The garden wakes and the grass stirs in unison.
Leaves start cladding the trees,
And butterflies flit like poetry in motion.

Snowdrops in abundance and tulips bursting forth,
Rainbow of flowers scattered all around.
Lakes warm up and fish come alive,
Splashing of colour covers the ground.

The Seasons

Golden globe rages, bringing warmth to all.
Bees get busy visiting flowers,
Birds are all around chirping merrily.
Trees laden with leaves stand proud at all hours.

Children gather at the beach, frolicking on the sand,
Lovers go around clutching each other's hands.
Seaside buzzes with tourists galore,
People soak in the sun clamouring for more.

Sun is at its zenith – the temperature soars,
Clouds come together and the thunder roars.
Streaks of lightning emblazons the sky
The rain splatters down from way up high.

Parched earth is soaked with clear nectar
Rivers rise up and overflow the rocky terrain
Boys and Girls dance in the rain.
Trees hold water and leaves drip to the ground
Birds sing and frogs croak all around.

Dry winds are no longer there to harass
Cool breeze now comes and is there to caress
Heat has gone – the soil is replete
Drops of rain drips, making the cycle complete.

A warm smile that always lights up the eyes,
The animated chat which gets interrupted by sighs.
Beautifully sculpted face framed by silky hair,
Glowing satin skin reminds one of an angel fair.
Elegant stance with a sway in the walk,
A spell is cast by the interesting talk.
Recounting tales of holiday with the fun she had,
Enjoying life even if it meant doing things which were slightly mad.
Going on walks in the serene countryside,
Spending time with friends and feeling thrilled.
Delving into family history with emotion and pride,
And when she is one with nature she feels fulfilled.
A spark appears when her eyes she crinkles,
A warmth spreads when her nose she wrinkles.
The atmosphere brightens by her lilting laugh,
And sadness in the heart is immediately reduced by half.
When she feels the pain her eyes do mist,
Her soul gets squeezed and tears pour into the eyes.
You want to reach out, hold her hand and insist,
That the pain will be fleeting if there is strength in the love ties.
You come by your soulmate once in a lifetime,
What triggers it- Logic- can't explain the mystery.
Good looks, husky voice, hourglass figure can be put forward as reasons sublime,
But it all boils down to the unfathomable human chemistry.

Soulmate

26

Life is hard, rude and stark,
Can deal a rough hand to even a bright spark.
Success and fame are your fair-weather friend,
Money and riches, you will soon spend.
Youth and good looks are also transitory,
Power and influence do come and go.
Talent with flair is a divine combination,
If you have it then it should be up for show.
Love and affection for one who is close to the heart,
Always thinking and caring even when torn apart.
Wanting the best for your love at your expense,
Genuinely wishing they peak sans pretense.
Right from the start, life - in the pit of the stomach - is the hard knot,
Colleagues judge you often while friends judge you not.
One-upmanship is played without shame,
They all say they do it for altruistic reasons,
When actually scoring a point is foremost in their mental frame.
Working life on the whole is usually mundane,
Success comes only once in a while.
Monotony is the name of the game,
With the occasional appreciation blossoming into a smile.

Children while growing up give you joy untold,
Then when they step into teenage years, be prepared for pain.
Arguments and tantrums is what they stick to and hold,
Once beyond those years they become human again.
Retirement then looms ahead and should be prepared for without strife,
Work should not be the sole purpose of life.
Work is the means to an end and living life to the full should be the goal,
Work should not overpower and cripple the soul.
This gift of life will only come once your way,
How long will it last, how long will it stay.
No one knows the answer and even prophets have fallen short.
Enjoy it today, don't wait for tomorrow,
For once you see it slipping through, all it leaves is regret and sorrow.

Life

Jammu simmering, Srinagar burning
Secessionists demanding independence.

Conducting their actions with impunity, at a level unheard,
"Hindutva" denigrated as a swear word.

The largest democracy held at ransom,
By the "fundamentalists" who are the new "Samson".

Innocent Muslims everywhere feel the people's ire
Searching for their identity through the cultural maze,
While the separatists spout venom and fire
With the opportunistic politicians consolidating their vote bank
by engineering a communalistic haze.

Kashmiris are reluctant Indians
Indians can never be Kashmiris

Article 370 imposed, so that Kashmiri hearts could be won,
Kashmiris have all the rights, Indians have none.

Justice and equality have no boundary,
Religion is an article of faith- God's path.
For the Muslims - "Haj" is paramount,
For the Hindu - it is "Amarnath".

Our political masters have a separate agenda and this is a fact
How to manipulate the minority to keep their position intact.

The common man is uncommon, his heart is big, his vision great.
He can tread the path of truth,
which in trying times can be narrow and straight.

India should be for Indians and not for a special religion, caste or creed.
The man on the street has to rally support to counter the politicians' greed.

From the crest of Himalaya to Kanniyakumari
From Gandhian Porbandar to mighty Bengal,
The single slogan which should resound through the entire land.
Is that all Indians are equal and there should be one law for all.

*Written at Ranchi, India after witnessing the disturbances in Srinagar
and Jammu in August 2008 when I had gone to visit Amarnath.*

Love is always thinking of the other,
Never worrying about your own pain.
Performing little acts from one day to another,
Concealing your lover's weaknesses and to never complain.
It is the thoughts that count,
With deeds following soon after .
At times when life's pressure can mount,
Your support and a cheerful word can turn frowns into laughter.
Love is anticipation,
Of what the other does desire.
Even for little things give genuine appreciation,
Go out of your way and their qualities you should admire.
When you go away and she is distraught,
You make gestures which she does not expect.
Bring even a small gift that shows her that she was in your thought,
You not only love her, but also her emotions you respect.
Love is forgiving and never holding a grudge,
Always forgetting the tears and remembering the smile.
If one forgets an important date then to just give a nudge,
Never rub it in as they might be feeling fragile.

The physical intimacy does initially excite,
But with time the electricity will disappear.
Just sitting together holding hands is such a delight,
Chatting away about nothing in particular,
does fill you with cheer.
Love reigns supreme on an emotional plane,
Once hooked, then it is there forever.
Nothing matters but caring thoughts for
each other, that remain,
Once you are soulmates the bond never
does sever.

Love

The sun scorches the land
The earth cracks up in pain
The grass is all burnt up
The animals look for water in vain.

Hot mist shimmers in the distance
Heat wave leads to unending strife
Clouds gather with thunder rumbling
The rain sweeps down rejuvenating life.

Light showers are so pleasant,
Refreshing and kind
Lovers holding hands, dancing in the rain
Soaking in the pleasure without a care in mind
Clutching on to ideals, having thoughts humane.

The gypsy's cardboard box goes soft as marshmallow
His humble abode is drowned in a pool shallow
His worldly possessions are stripped bare to the bone.
He is hungry, wet and cold;
From his lips escape a moan.

The rain is now relentless
The skies are dark, blanketing the moon's glow
Waters incessant percussion
With canals flooding and the rivers overflow.

The water keeps on rising threatening one's home
Roads become rivers with whirlpools of turbulent foam
Lives are lost and you can hear the people's groan
Water has now changed its guise
From the life-giving creator
It is now leading to people's demise.

The Rains

Thoughts are the scaffolding on which words are built,
But sans action, words are hollow.
Thoughts on their own are a waste of time and can lead to
guilt,
Marry actions to words and celebration will follow.

Silent thoughts are the foam on waves,
Here today, gone tomorrow.
Words not culminating in action,
Are the root cause of many a sorrow.

Time is relentless even for the Kingly crown
Never comes back, never slows down.

If then you miss the boat,
By keeping words under cover and thoughts under a shroud.
With expressions in a deep moat,
And actions under a cloud

Hark - hold still - and remember the proverb you have heard.
That actions always speak louder than the word.

Thoughts, Words and Deeds

The seagulls circled, the waves splashed,
Mountains towered with their peaks with clouds capped.
The ship was anchored with the crew eager and ready,
Excited passengers clambered up holding on to the rails to keep steady.
The luggage had reached the rooms, the cabins were neat and compact,
One just needed to settle in and have the suitcases unpacked.
Then there were the welcome drinks and the invite to sample the gourmet food,
In the spacious lounge we all mingled and enjoyed, as the atmosphere was so good.
Night descended and reluctantly we did retire,
For the adrenaline was pumping and our imagination was on fire.
In the mind's eye visions of icebergs floated, adorned by penguins galore,
We drifted off to sleep and were only awoken by the sound of the ocean's roar.
Looking out of the window we saw the giant waves of the Drake passage,
The ship was tossed about but to its route it did keep to manage.
Once out of the oceanic confluence, there descended a gentle calm,
White glazed mountains leaned across the ice strewn sea, as if to impalm.
The ship negotiated through the carpet of ice,
Progress was slow while the breathtaking scenery did entice.
A solitary emperor penguin stood majestically on the slab of white,
Leopard seals languidly relaxed with an inner delight.
The albatross rode the skies with imperial grace,
The killer whales beat the ship by their astonishing pace.

Gentoo penguins followed a narrow path up the iced slope without commotion,
Tabular icebergs rocked gently in the blue ocean.
Skuas hovered overhead looking for a chance to pick up a penguin chick,
The penguin parents huddled together and fed their young, without missing a trick.
Terns, petrels and gulls nested on the cliff face,
Leaving periodically for food and the same path they would retrace.
The Adélie looked you in the eye with their flippers slightly bent,
While the Chinstraps porpoised in the sea to their hearts content.
The Gentoo male picked up a pebble or two and offered it to his mate,
Helping to build a nest for the precious offspring , walking his special gait.
Sunsets came late, the white was splashed with yellow,

The White Kingdom

Humpback whales rose in unison producing a sound that was mellow.
Moonrise over the icebergs was a scintillating sight,
Twinkling stars and shimmering reflection did poetry in me ignite.
Kayaking on your own in the blue white expanse,
Hearing the sounds of silence left you in a trance.
The majesty of the mountains, the pristine ice,
The golden painted skies by the splash of sunrise.
The music of the birds, the lapping of the waves,
A bluish hue shone forth from within the iceberg caves.
Antarctica is paradise, its heaven and earth rolled into one,
A trip to this magical kingdom will your senses it will stun.

It fills you with awe, it is out of this world,
Once you have been there your mind gets twirled.
It is poetry, it is a painting, it is the eternal fable,
It's white, it's pure, it's unforgettable.

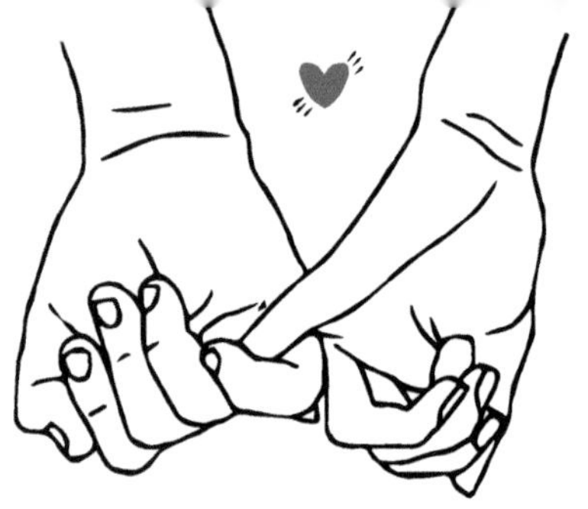

Promises and mutterings of love describing the pangs of absence,
Are mere words and words have no permanence.
Relationships come and go and what was professed to last a lifetime,
Falls short with "forever" finishing off on occasions in months six to nine.
There is a time when lovers can't bear to part,
Then comes a time when they would rather be apart.
You feel empty when the phone does not ring,
Soon enough the ring of the phone becomes overpowering.
A day would not pass when you would not yearn to hear his voice,
Now stopping it altogether is your choice.
You make him feel special in a class of his own,
Then other things take precedence and then him you disown.
A dream castle is built which in thought the two of you have graced,
Then he becomes redundant and so is replaced.
Forever remaining soulmates was the mantra being spoke,
Now there is someone else in tow so the first attachment is broke.
Often mentioned was being one with each other in this life and the next,
Then soon contact has to be minimal and what is the point of sending a text.
Life is like that, with highs and lows,
Lovers sighing like Shakespeare's furnace.
Initially madly in love and always on the go,
Then fate intervenes and then he seems more of a menace.

Love is cyclical - the eternal chain,
Even if you are prepared you feel the pain.
The peaks and troughs should be taken in their stride,
For the incorrigible lover, it is better to have loved and lost than to have Love never tried.

Love Lost

It is the waiting that wrenches your heart
It is the waiting that tears you apart,
It is the waiting, hoping that the phone will ring
It is the hoping, waiting for the engagement to turn into a wedding ring.

The postman's footfall on the gravel
Walking laboriously the beaten trail,
One always continues to marvel
How instead of a love letter all you get is junk mail.

The birthday celebration
The feeling of exhilaration
Friends and family arrive
Cutting the cake after blowing out the candle
Gifts galore pile up on the table.

But to understand it is difficult and hard
Why your lady love did not send a birthday card
Valentine Day comes and goes
No cards or gifts materialise,
She says she really cares for you
One of these days there will be a pleasant surprise.

Christmas is coming near
you hope it will bring cheer
Get you a token of love from someone dear
But its absence fills you with fear
She said she was thinking of you, giving her reaction
The words remain empty and never transform into action.

Waiting has anticipation
Which can be tinged with apprehension.
If waiting is rewarded by neglect
And care is thrown to the winds.
Then your emotions you must try and conserve.
For your love she does not deserve.

Anticipation

Colours of Nature

To the sun waking up, it's his fiery crimson chariot that matters,
The black veil of night is then soon shred to tatters.
Silver stars that studded the kohl night sky,
Go hide themselves when the golden dawn saunters by.
Green leaves sway in the cool breeze,
Thick brown branches herald the majesty of trees.
Violet lilacs wink in the morning sun,
Pink-cheeked children go outdoors to have some fun.
The red rose for lovers leaves no emotional dearth,
The blue sky offers a roof to the entire earth.
Come autumn and the leaves have gone yellow,
After grey thunder the weather has turned mellow.
Lavender flowers entice the bees at random,
Myriad coloured butterflies dance in the garden with gay abandon.
An orange carpet lines the ground during the fall,
Bluish gold peacocks strut around proud and tall.
White snowflakes float lazily to the ground,
While ruby flamingos produce their melodious sound.
Nature - the artist, displays itself, splashing colours for show,
The heavens light up, after the rains, and paint a stunning rainbow.

Pulak Sahay

Lightning crackled, thunder roared,
Winds blew and clouds soared.
The sun then joined in and played with mirth,
Encouraging the raindrops to race to the earth.
The cracked caked soil longed for the sprinkle,
Raindrops soon soaked in smoothing the lands wrinkle.
With the monsoon pouring down, the raindrops seep through,
Rivulets become rivers and lakes form too.
Parched trees welcome the respite and lap up the moisture,
Dry leaves having drunk to their full regain their lustre.
The sun beats down warming up the air,
To dissipate the heat the leaves spread out while still in the sun's glare.
Raindrops rise blissfully and soon become the cloud,
The breeze blows it higher and the heavens get curtained in a shroud.
The silvery foam rides joyously in the sky,
Sunrays dance all over and peek at the eagles flying by.
Day turns to night when the sun does finally flee,
The temperature plummets while the stars shine with glee.
The thunder then rumbles and clouds gyrate,
In lightning-lit skies the drops of rain aggregate.
The firmament darkens and can't hold on to the rain,
Raindrops splatter down completing the age-old cyclical chain.

Life History of Raindrops

The first sliver of sunlight makes a rent in the curtain dark,
The birds stir in their nests and start singing in unison.
The wind emboldens and nudges the mighty oak, making its mark,
The sky is splashed red as the sun has finally woken.
The glittering stars that adorned the night sky,
Observed the pristine clouds that gently floated by.
As the sun then rose over the earth with pride,
The swaggering stars of the night, in the morn, did bashfully hide.
The bees plunged vigorously into their daily chore,
The flowers preened themselves hoping for an encore.
The butterflies flitted from one blossom to the next,
The eagles rearranged their nests over the tree's crest.
The squirrels rushed about gathering every nut,
The peacock in regal splendour do in the forest strut.
The rabbits come out of their burrows and munch on the juicy leaf,
The horse chestnut spreads its branches in the sun offering shade and welcome relief.
The sun is past its prime and moves gently to the west,
God's creatures, after a burst of activity, are now wanting to take rest.
Heat is ebbing and a breeze is starting to blow,
Shadows start to lengthen and the sky begins to glow.

From golden yellow the blue is now burning red,
The seagulls, after a hard day's work, are returning to their brood.
The foam of the splashing waves, over the rocks, has gradually spread,
The weary fishermen return looking at the shore with gratitude.
Dusk has arrived and the horizon is on fire,
The bubbling energy of dawn which initially did inspire.
Finishes off with Nature now running its course, with its trough and peak,
After vibrant life, decay sets in, with the inevitable end being bleak.
Life is cyclical with its ups and downs,
Laughter and sadness affects even the kingly crown.
So never lose heart or be forlorn,
For though night follows day, after dusk comes dawn.

Dawn and Dusk

The heavy curtains of night do steadily part
Bringing life to colours that flowers adorn,
Warming the earth and people's hearts
Golden globe shines and dawn is born.

Soaks up the dew
Makes fluffy cloud,
Creates the rainbow hue
Strutting peacocks in the jungle are proud.

Encourages the seeds to shoot
With sunrays showering the land,
Helps the trees to leaf and fruit
There is a sparkle in the eye of sand.

Thaws the snow,
Ushers in the spring
Spurs the birds to hop and sing,
Brings a satin glow to lover's cheek
Children go out and play hide and seek.

Have seen many a times standing on the shore,
The king of daylight riding chariots of fire,
Burning up during its relentless motion;

Come dusk when darkness starts to pour,
It pauses and before it does retire
Cools down by taking a dip in the ocean.

Globe of Fire

The black curtain of night envelopes the sky,
As soon as daylight fades, darkness slithers by.
The sun retires after a hectic day,
Birds return to their roost while crickets come out to play.
Steadily the stars light up the night dome,
Crisscross the firmament adorning their home.
Like a jewelled canopy that sparkles with bliss,
Enthuses lovers to hold hands and steal a kiss.
Starlight quivers poking through the cloud,
Winking at each other with mischief in their eye.
While newlyweds profess their love clear and loud,
Promising eternal togetherness accompanied with a deep sigh.
The moon sits serene among its fellow stars,
Bathing the sparkling bodies in moon glow.
While the cuckoo sings admiring it from afar,
Pining in love, hoping for a better tomorrow.
The shooting star catches the eye of lovers,
They hold on to each other and make a wish.
Oblivious of the world that can be cruel and heartless,
Praying that all their problems do finally vanish.

Night advances and stillness has gradually spread,
The atmosphere is serene and wind has died down.
The radiance of the twinkling stars has become widespread,
The dozing earth is drenched in a starlit gown.
Day breaks and the gold of sun streaks,
The silvery stars in the expanse of blue hide.
The ocean wakes up and seagulls do shriek,
The east has gone red like a blushing bride.
Stars in the skies play hide and seek,
Here tonight gone in the morrow.
Dazzle the world with their beauty unique,
Gladden poet's hearts mitigating their perennial sorrow.

Jewels in the Sky

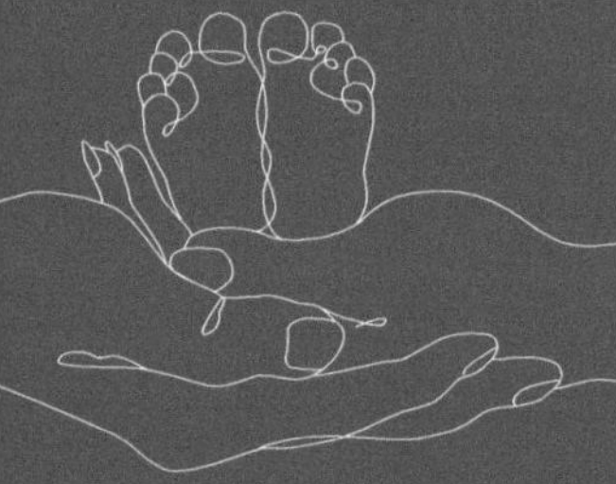

The ides of March came by,
Rainbows adorned the sky.
Butterflies flitted and Robins sang,
Lilting music of early spring rang.
Family and friends did sway in the morn,
Our first grandchild, had just been born.

An angel with a delightful smile,
Twinkling eyes that had the depth of a mile.
Gurgling sounds like a musical symphony,
The tiny soul gave us untold bliss, as we looked at her wistfully.

Weeks grew and into months became ,
Our lives transformed and we were no longer the same.
There was not only joy but always an earnest desire,
Getting down to London to see Eila was what we did require.

She started to crawl, she would endlessly babble.
Parents and "Mozi Med" revelled in her cackle.
Eila was the celebrity,
Mum the photographer extraordinaire.
Grandad was rejuvenated and would hold her in his lap with great care.

Then one day she stood up and effortlessly walked,
Like a trapeze artist with her arms in the air,
We were all so pleasantly shocked,
But more so her mum who felt that Eila had a natural flair,
And was a rambler beyond compare.

The ides of March have come again but are not gone,
Eila has reached the magical birthday figure of number one.
She mouths "Dada" and "Mama",
and we are hoping for "Mozi" and "Nana".

So do listen intently and soak up the atmosphere,
As she dances to music and lights up the room with her eyes,
For her birthday today is being celebrated by VIPs, including the Sun
and the Stars in the skies.

Eila Anamsa

Written for the first birthday of our first grandchild

I never wanted to be a doctor as my mother was one, I do recall,
She was always busy and away on call.
Looking after patients, never finding time to rest,
Missing meals but still working with zest.

Then she climbed the ladder and became more senior,
Busy operating and teaching her juniors.
Regularly gave lectures and was in-charge of her ward,
Sought after by all as by her patients she was adored.

When she walked in the hospital, her team had to run,
She was always on the move, pushing herself to get the work done.
She clambered up the stairs and her registrars would pant,
Keeping up with her was not an easy job - I do grant.

She was the Professor, the doyen of her speciality,
If you wanted the best care, she offered quality.
The whole town reverberated with her name,
Trust, hard work and honesty were the names of her game.

Then came the end of an era and she retired,
She was still in peak form and was never tired.
Her work continued and patients still did flock,
She worked from home and her home did rock.

Her aura had overpowered me and my ambition had changed,
I now wanted to be a doctor as my thought process had been rearranged.
Wanting to emulate her was my sole aim,
So I worked hard to match her commitment and ensured my ethics remained the same.

Time took its toll and she slowed down,
Very gradually, although her name remained, there was competition in town.
There were younger, more enthusiastic doctors on the rise,
That she was getting old and not having the energy to compete, was no surprise.

Her joints started to creak and the painful movement she could not ignore,
Getting up from the chair was a real chore.
She would hobble and walk at a slow pace,
There was need for a helping hand or a stick on the staircase.

My Mother

Joint replacement did give her a new lease of life,
Mobility returned and movement was no longer a strife.
But ageing is relentless and never does stop,
The mind can remain swift but the body is a flop.

My mother today of four score and four,
Is a distant cry from the super swift doctor of 1984.
She limps, she groans, she gets up with pain,
She needs aids, she needs help, life is a constant strain.

I now want to look after my mother,
The way she looked after me.
The way her ethical principles, in me, she did inspire,
And instilled a sense of purpose to help others less fortunate,
Is what I most admire.

I am now a grandfather and have fulfilled my dream,
Been a doctor and teacher and worked full steam.
Retirement is now on the horizon and soon I will be free,
And I hope my children follow my example,
And in my old age, look after me.

Wrote after seeing my mum very ill and frail in India in June 2012

I am so lucky, I feel so good,
My lady loves me, like she should.
I am plain and she is gorgeous,
There is no comparison between the two of us.
Twinkling eyes, cascading hair,
Tinkling laughter, complexion so fair.
Swan neck and cheeks with a dimple,
Seductive body and yet so simple.
She doesn't say much, she controls her emotion,
She has a calming effect on me, through life's commotion.
A tiny gesture from her goes a long way,
It thrills my soul, whatever anyone might say.
Her picture is indelibly etched in my heart,
She will always be mine even though we might be apart.
Our love is ethereal, so delicate, so pure,
Which is why I can't live without her, about that I am sure.

I Am So Lucky

Midnight chimes six decades and seven years ago ushered in joy, trust and hope,
India was free, but with problems of poverty and population the government had to cope.
Blood, sweat and tears of millions had ultimately borne fruit,
To the "Loh Purush", Bapu and his heir, everyone did salute.

India was to be the new "Utopia",
Five Year plans were designed.
Heavy industries established,
Development plans to bureaucrats assigned.

Hindi-Chini Bhai-Bhai was the mantra spoken,
Peace and non-violence were our slogan.
Bharat on the world stage was non-aligned,
Then from across the Chinese border, attack came and Pandit Ji's health declined.

Emotional treachery had taken its toll,
By this "unkindest cut of all".
The rose on the lapel withered, the spirit faded,
Only the outer shell remained, though thoroughly jaded.

Supporting India in this trying time,
Came the "Big man" in the small frame,
Extolling the virtues of the Jawan and the Kisan,
Honesty was his creed, simplicity his middle name.
Fate, however at Tashkent was particularly cruel,
As following "Bahadur's" funeral in India there started a dynastic rule.

Time flowed by and governance took a big hit,
Nepotism and corruption flourished and democracy disintegrated bit by bit.
The only time in independent India's history was the country under a yoke,
"Emergency" had been clamped and people's voices were choked.

No one it seemed could lead India out of this mess,
The "Anuj" was the heir apparent and India his largesse.
"Bharat Mata" was a hostage to the Amma's clan,
Following the plane crash the political mantle was draped on the "pilot", with elan.

India Wins Freedom Again

When the "Absolute leader" was shot, following the desecration of the Golden temple conclave,
The "Jyestha putra" took over charge, riding a sympathy wave.
But "Mr. Clean" got tainted by Bofors,
It was alleged that he was filling his coffers.
Then whether it was the "Linguist" or the "Silent Sikh" at the helm,
It was because "Italy Ki Beti" had allowed them to rule over the realm.
The dynasty ruled, with Madam wielding extra constitutional powers, leading to disruption,
The economy faltered and rampant raged corruption.
The public was frustrated, dejected and in a rage,
It was only a matter of time when this "tiger" in the common man would come out of the cage.

While India was struggling the "saffron" politicians who ruled Gujarat decided, it be sorted,
So the "RSS pracharak" was sent there to ensure that the people were supported.
The "Gujarati bhai" took on the reins of power,
Gujarat then became "vibrant" and prosperity on it, did shower.
He was the man whose "Ekta yatra" went from Srinagar to Kanniyakumari,
And the philosophy of Hindutva was woven into the fabric of all and sundry.

But then a haze descended on this "nationalist" at "Godhra", as the "Kar Sevaks" were burned,
The fallout was the riots, which to this day have led the "secular" media to have him spurned.
These "holier than thou" intellectuals don't mention the three score riots, that remain a slur
on India's humanity,
Or that half of them were perpetrated on India's majority,
For them the anti-Sikh riots never happened and only "Godhra" is the insanity.

No one dare mention the ethnic cleansing of the Kashmiri Pandits in their scores,
As maintaining Article 370 and abrogating Article 44 keeps the vote banks secure.
This disciple of Vivekanand was however unfazed, as he was a worker par excellence,
Working non-stop for Gujarat and caring for all, led to his eminence.
"Sadbhavna" mission was taken on with relentless energy,
"GIFT" to Gujarat and India was the International communities' envy.

Development for all was the buzz word for the entire state,
It was non-stop progress that made Gujarat look great.
This, while India was struggling and growth rate was down, with inflation on the rise,
The ruling first family was callous in their attitude towards the masses, and just looked to the skies.

When the 2014 general elections knocked on the door,
The mother and son took it for granted, thinking they had won the ballot war.
The fight was on,
The battle lines were drawn,
It was a clash of the titans,
Between the plebeians and the patricians.
There ensued a David-Goliath battle,
And against the "Vikas Purush", the "Yuvraj" did crumble.

Hindus, Sikhs, Christians and Muslims are all first Indians, in a manner of speak,
Separating them to "divide and rule" has been the age old technique.
The Indian public is discerning, clear-headed and wise,
When the crunch comes they can separate truth from lies.
So the "Gujarat Ratna" in the 16th Lok Sabha elections, got a thumping majority,
His slogan of "Sabka Saath, Sabka Vikas" stirred the hearts of the Indian society.

The magical figure of 272 was crossed and the "man of the moment" seemed to have a halo,
The "Ganchi" proved himself and did drub the "Kashmiri Pandit family" hollow.
The political gurus and secular stalwarts were all proven wrong,
People were sick of empty words and failed promises and wanted prosperity.
The days of vote bank of caste and religion were over,
And the crying need was development and progress by ensuring peace and unity.

Now India is set to forge ahead in the 21st century,
The world is looking at India with anticipation and bated breath,
People want to be identified as Indians, whether they come from Gujarat or Bengal,
And the universal slogan that is resounding through the entire land, is that,
All Indians are equal and there should be one law for all.

Indians have this time reposed immense faith in the "Chaiwallah",
For they are confident, like Mahabharat's Arjun, that they have on their side the "Invincible Gwala".

Written on the 16th of May 2014 when Mr. Narendra Modi won the 16th Lok Sabha elections.
Revised on 31st of May on the advice of Lord Bhikhu Parekh.
Also followed some suggestions of my friends on 14th of June.
(GIFT= Gujarat International Finance Tech City)
(Invincible Gwala= Lord Krishna)

White cloak of winter envelopes trees, roads and stream,
The young ones get invigorated, and running around, they let off their steam.
As day turns to dusk and spills into premature night,
With opaque skies, there is no Sun in sight.

A haze descends, fog ascends,
And cars headlights struggle to pierce the blanched curtain.
Temperature plummets with commuters on the road, snaking their way,
Latching on to the tail lights in front, as of their way they are uncertain.

While parents struggle in the inclement weather, but still go out to work,
to earn their daily bread.
Children are oblivious and delight when the snowflakes patter on their head.
Their joy knows no bound, when there is more of snow to play around.

From the warm interior of double glazed homes, winter is pretty and can adorn a frozen lake,
Out in the cold when the wind bites in, the poetry of winter disappears,
leaving only shivers in its wake.
When the temperature is down, the snow looks pristine,
On melting, the mirage disappears, and the slush appears, which looks unclean.

The sludge and sleet make the roads icy and treacherous,
Accidents are only a blink away and going out in the snow, no longer seems adventurous.

Snow and ice masquerade with masks galore,
With angelic beauty on the outside, and dirt within the core.
Better the sandy plains, and muddy river bank,
The rustic honesty of summer, with the Sun pulling rank.

The sweat on the brow, and glistening perspiration,
The brown of the dirt, and earthy imagination.
Winter and summer are flip sides of the coin,
The east and west that never do meet.
The winter white, with its cold exterior, can plunge moods into a dark gloom,
But with the summer's sun lighting up the skies, spirits light up, and the earth does bloom.

Icy Winter

The political analysts are incisive and bright,
And go the extra mile to predict electoral outcomes - all verified.
They feel that the common man can be taken for a ride,
As he is poor and uneducated and willing to be bribed.

Restricted by caste and religion, and vision narrow-minded,
Unwilling or unable to see beyond the tip of their nose - just short-sighted.
At their peril they realise that the common man is the heart and soul of Bharat,
Whether they come from Arunachal or Gujarat.

The man on the street feels the pulse of the political leaders, who wield their might,
Going beyond the sound bite and the frilly shows and ascertaining what is right.
Peering through the political haze, they are never fazed,
They have proved their mettle time and again.

It was Pandit Ji's honesty and dedication that kept him in power,
When his daughter faltered then they did not think twice and her time was over.
Brought her back when the Janta Dal among themselves quarrelled,
Gave an opportunity to BJP who for power had then jostled.

When India did not shine for all Indians, Congress was once again in the saddle,
With corruption and cronyism rampant,
the Vikas Purush was given the nation's boat through troubled waters to paddle.
But with development not trickling down quickly enough to the masses,
The "Mufflerman" was given a hoist by the have-nots and the middle classes.

The Aam Aadmi is not "Aam" at all but is "Khaas",
For they are discerning on a pan-nationalistic scale and can political gurus surpass.
A castigation of the Indian junta has been their predilection for slavery,
How they tend to fawn over Royalty and vote for the "family" as opposed to quality.

But observe the fate of the Congress in the Lok Sabha elections of last year,
and the Delhi elections of today,
And by the same token the BJP has also been taught a stinging lesson straightaway.
The take home message is, to not take the "Aam" public for granted,
Humility and delivery to the population at large, is the definitive mantra
on which success is founded.

As otherwise the judgement passed in the Janta durbar,
Will have you enthroned today, and gone tomorrow, lost in the bazaar.
No one party or person is sacrosanct,
Only results count and honesty remains top ranked.

*Started writing after AAP had their landslide victory
in the Delhi elections on 10th February 2015*

Young and dashing and full of verve,
Off to the office on his pushbike, while maintaining his reserve.
He had 2 sets of clothes which he washed and himself did iron,
Never was the white ever dull, nor a crease out of turn.

He had come from a distant village, and was self-taught in all his ways,
He worked hard for himself and his family, and did trail a blaze.
A man of modest means, who looked to the skies,
Life had been his teacher, and he was eminently streetwise.

In his younger days he had even managed a pub, whose atmosphere was dank,
But inspite of his youth and young friends, he never smoked or drank.
He had big ideas for his family, his wife and his son,
In the spring of his life, he had plans on how things should be done.

A man who detested regimented subordination, decided to quit the police,
He wanted to be treated as an equal, and so joined the civil service.
He steadily climbed the ladder, with hard work and tenacity, as his only recourse,
For his son he had the best school in mind, which was way beyond his resource.

Spring turned to summer, and years did roll,
His doctor wife became a lecturer, and son into the medical college did enroll.
This self-made man with no safety net was struck with Tuberculosis and was bed-ridden,
But even then for his son's career there was never any dimming of his vision.

A man who had always lived in a rented apartment,
Built his own house and that made him feel buoyant.
Ages ago he had been chided for dreaming of buying in the capital, a piece of land,
Soon enough the dream turned into reality, when on his property, he built a house that was grand.

His wife became a professor and daughter a doctor,
His son's wife and son-in-law were also medics and according to his philosophy,
bid comfort adieu.
In the autumn of his life, his post was that of a commissioner,
A man who had started at the bottom, now by all counts,
had reached a stage that looked brighter.

Papa and the Seasons

Still he kept stimulating his children to achieve a higher goal,
Now that the grandchildren were around, his goading took on a new role.
The first time he went abroad was when his son's age was a score and a decade,
Even while holidaying abroad, his aim was to organise things for his son,
so that he would get some accolade.

His son in UK became a consultant and daughter-in-law a GP in the National Health Service,
His daughter and her husband chose USA as their abode, where their work was endless.
In his winter years, when he was 4 scores old,
This sprightly man of yesteryears fell and fractured his hip and suffered pain untold.
But with true grit and a stoic face, he limped on and did his daily chore,
The body gradually gave in, but the mind remained alert and laziness he did abhor.

The end came swiftly and he did not linger on,
One day after we had joked and chatted at night, he fell ill and 3 days later, he was gone.
I distinctly remember that August day, when while the Sun was out,
the inside of the house turned bleak and cold.
As if winter had come prematurely, and taken hold of my father, who had suddenly become old.

The day before, my father was alive and I was his son,
Then he was gone and I had instantaneously become an orphan.
But such is life and what comes must go,
His thoughts and deeds remain and will forever glow.
I try not to shed a tear when I am alone,
As it would be a disservice to his memory, if I wept even when I was on my own.

I therefore do not remember him as the elderly man in the wheelchair,
But rather the dapper young man with sleek dark combed hair.
The man whose wit was sharp and who was quick on the repartee,
Someone who was thoroughly dependable, and who would take on the next challenge with glee.

Though physically my father is no more,
His spirit remains, and he guides me just as before.
When I think of him, the cold of autumn and winter shrink aside,
And the fresh warmth of spring and summer engulfs me and I feel gratified.

Wrote this poem while sitting in my painting room thinking about my father who died in 2008

When sadness wrings the heart, the tears get squeezed out,
Eyes well up and down the cheek does it slide.
Once the tears are spent, the weight over the heart is lifted,
And hence it always feels light, once you have cried.

Happiness triggers the fountain in the soul,
As if a sprinkler is switched on, and over the face, do crystal
balls roll.
Heralding joy to people far and near,
Such tears are infectious, and spread easily amongst friends
and family, who are very dear.

T e a r s

When frustration strikes and you feel powerless and impotent,
When all your efforts slither down the grease pole.
Only tears remain, with your soulmate, preventing you from banging your head
against a brick wall.
Even when you feel encompassed by a black hole.

Then there is the time when you don't need enemies, as "friends" take over that task,
For ulterior motives, they stab you in the back.
For petty gains they dole out hurt, which stings like salt water on a bruise,
And soon out of the eyes, the same water does ooze.

In the hectic pace of life, when there are not enough hours in the day,
Strain builds up, and finally tiredness holds its sway.
Fatigue sets in and the body is under pressure,
That is the time, when before slumber kicks in, the tears spill out and soothe its owner.

Achieving your goal,
Attaining your dream.
Makes you feel proud,
And with joy you want to scream.

Your chest swells up and you stand tall,
As that droplet of fluid from the eye does fall.
Intense emotion of any kind,
Something that stokes the heart and caresses the soul.

Like acts of courage, honesty and sacrifice,
Qualities on which you can't put a price.
That is when the oyster of the eye, conjures up a pearl,
And after crossing the lower eyelid, down does it involuntarily hurl.

The teardrop hides a palette, consisting of hues galore,
Composed of various facets made of joy, pride and valour.
Mixed with hurt, sadness and frustration,
Like colours of the rainbow, when in a mix it is spun,
Turning out a pristine white, at its culmination.
Tears are the currency, used by the heart and soul,
Laden with myriads of emotion, in people, one and all.

It was a long way from home, leaving friends and family behind,
Overcoming racial differences and adopting practices of cultures, belonging to an alien humankind.
Rising through the ranks, using sweat and toil,
Remembering your roots and the purpose of the turmoil.

Constantly concentrating to make a future of your own,
Giving a boost to the family and for your children a stepping stone.
Then when you have arrived and the children are on the right track,
You think of home and consider going back.

You want to repay the debt you owe your home nation,
Contribute your might, turning your job into a vocation.
Help the less fortunate in getting a foot up the ladder,
That is when reality check hits you, and you progress from being sad to getting sadder.

Nobody is interested in the knowledge that you can contribute,
Or the help you can give them to better themselves by perseverance and labour,
They are content if it is monies you can distribute,
And please do save the lecture about honesty and hard work.
For this is not England, and hence they ask you to tell it to the birds or to their next door neighbour.

Pravasi Bharatiya Diwas takes place in January each year,
On the anniversary of the Mahatma's return from South Africa.
But all you ever hear are pompous empty words,
with Bapu's ethos being the current politicians anathema.
It started with good thoughts but the "karma" is missing,
Live blogging and Tweeting has become the order of the day,
With no concern about raising the common Indian's standard of living.

Just like the environment the politicians minds are polluted,
Using caste and religion as loaded dice, they feign honesty.
Working to uplift the downtrodden, for them, is a travesty,
And the fact that their core is putrid is undisputed.

Pravasi Bharatiya
Overseas Indian

Lofty slogans jar the ear, and make you cringe inside,
While the thick-skinned "neta" has through his teeth, repeatedly lied.
Invoking leaders names from their dynastic families, with dubious reputation,
And grinding the Lok Sabha to a halt, leading to India's depredation.

Not only is the traffic chaotic, it reflects in the administration too,
Even if you want routine work done, you either grease the palm
or join the back of the never ending queue.
There is no ownership, the system is rotten,
Dishonesty pervades every strata of society.
The Sardar Patel, Nehru and Shashtris have conveniently been forgotten,
And in their place has been enthroned the politician, noted for their notoriety.

Their ill gotten wealth and their criminal activities,
Go unpunished as they hold the nation to ransom, without any care.
And nothing will change unless literacy lights up the minds of the common man,
engendering responsibility,
As well as demanding from the "khakhi clad" that all work be done for people's welfare.

Till that day of the golden dawn, when India's GDP will match its social indicators,
The Pravasi Bharatiya will have to remain an NRI because of these political perpetrators.
And until the thought, word and deeds of India's leaders resonate in unison,
They will have to continue to work from foreign lands, for their Hindustan,
keeping it their life's sole mission.

Muslims killing Muslims in the name of Allah,
The Sunnis denigrating Shias and vice versa.
But attaining and holding on to power, is their real motive,
Religion is just a facade, but useful, as it makes people emotive.

Humans become animals akin to the mild mannered Langur turning into a Gorilla,
First it was Afghanistan, then Iraq and now it is Syria.
Civil war has been the order of the day, as highlighted by the media.
Atrocities are ladled out on all, without remorse,
No compassion, no morals, no rules - only brute force.

The political vacuum generates chaos and disorder,
And in this cauldron the human spirit gets cooked, and out spills the marauder.
The common man is always at the receiving end,
Whether it be Muslim, Christian or Jew, somebody's enemy or friend.

Everyday life is such a continuous torture,
That families round up what they have, and are ready for departure.
Men with their women and children, are willing to make the perilous journey into the unknown,
To leave the hell hole created by their co-religionists, and hope to re-establish their life all alone.
That is when the people smugglers, come into their own,
Taking advantage of people's misfortune, extracting money,
and then leaving them and their children to cry and groan.

Treading miles on sore feet, empty stomach and a heavy heart,
Hoping for a better future for families that have been torn apart.
It is then that they are confronted by the barbed wire,
As no politician's heart or wallet is big enough to cope with their own population's ire.

Bewildered children, helpless mothers and frustrated men are left to their cruel fate,
As fighters of Daesh go on to proclaim the Islamic Caliphate.
It is déjà vu as one gets reminded of the horrors of seven decades earlier,
The name and the religion of the perpetrators are different, but their heinous crimes are very similar.

The media are shouting the loudest proclaiming that free entry of refugees,
 is compassionate and a matter of conscience,
The politicians and the electorate on the ground, fear that as their own services are stretched,
Allowing in more bodies, flies in the face of reason and is nonsense.

Migrant Crisis

So the UK is opting out of the European refugee solution, where you are allocated a quota or number,
For Britain wants to support these migrants nearer their home,
so that the life of UK citizens is not encumbered.
Some argue that doubling the refugees allowed in, would help solve the problem,
What they don't realise is that the refugee trickle that started, is now a tsunami, ready to overwhelm.

Everyone you hear is in the fire fighting mode,
No one is willing to stop and think as to why it all started and how the migrant flow can be slowed.
Targeting the problem at source, would stem the flow of humankind,
And go a long way in resettling these unfortunates, with a sustainable pragmatic solution,
Which is also well designed.

In this third war of the world, it is the terrorist against the rest,
The sane world has to join hands, bury their petty differences and then pass the acid test.
This monster akin to the Third Reich has to be crushed and the evil erased,
As it is only then that from the ashes of disorder, the phoenix will rise again,
leading to good governance which is firmly based.

It is only then that this sorry saga will finally draw to a close,
With these migrants rehoused in their own homes,
in their own nation, attaining lasting peace and ultimate repose.

*Wrote this poem after constantly listening to the media, politicians (of all hues) and philanthropists who
Have the "Fire fighting" approach and keep on talking ceaselessly about increasing the number of refugees who
should be allowed entry into Europe, rather than wanting to solve or eradicate the cause of crisis.*

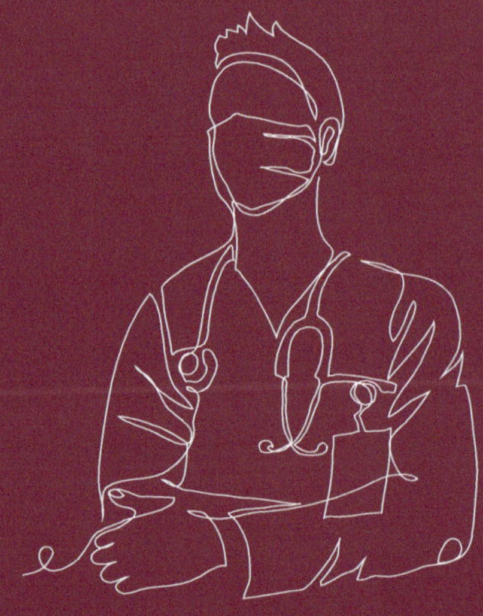

In the autumn of my life, I pause and cast a backward glance,
My life flashes past and I watch the teenaged Pulak dance.
Life was good as a schoolboy, with no mortgage worries or care,
Although at that time it did not seem so, as there was the important decision to make,
like choosing between the style of Elvis or the Beatle's hair.

This was in the spring of my life, when I had a spring in my step, you will understand,
I did feel immortal, as there was so much time on my hands.
Tennis, swimming and theatre took up most of my day,
What was left of the hours, I did fritter away.
But writing to my parents, I insisted, I was studying hard,
This in essence was a load of canard.

I was more interested in girls, drama and debate,
Studies came a poor fourth and so when I did not get into pre-med school, my father did me,
berate.
Good sense dawned and I had a change of heart,
Studies became my prime goal and hard work gave me a head start.

I did well at medical school and then did my postgraduate,
Soon it was time for greener pastures and to England I did emigrate.
I was already married and had 2 little girls to flaunt,
Then 6 years later my son was born whose personality, later on, spelt "nonchalant".

Autumn

We struggled, worked hard and fortune on us did smile,
Geeta became a GP and I, a Consultant, and life seemed worthwhile.
The children did show their mettle,
They have all gone down to London, to settle.
So Geeta and I live in this big house with a lovely canine,
Reminds me of the time when I left my parents, in a bigger house, as my life, I wanted to define.

This is the story of every household,
People buy big houses and make them even bigger,
Then the children depart and rooms get locked and cold,
And if you are not careful, then only babysitting makes you feel richer.

So do prepare in the summer of your life,
Think of how you will spend quality time with your wife.
Ultimately retirement does set you free,
But then if you are not careful, you soon feel, that you are out at sea.

However if you do not give in to expectation,
If you spend your money without reserve.
If you enjoy doing things on your own and with friends, achieving elation,
You will keep on going in your twilight years, with vigour and verve.

Then in your winter years, you will have no discontent,
If you take the final step forward and end the pursuit.
Of not only external pleasures, but of feelings within,
You would have achieved "nirvana" and become a "Buddha" to boot.

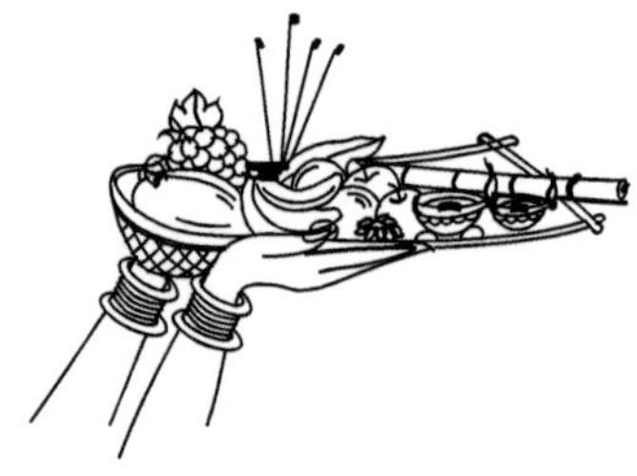

The Egyptians called it "Ra",
To the Indians it was Surya.
The Greeks addressed it as Helios,
For the Akkadians it was Shamash.

It gave joy and energy to the earth,
With the sun shining, life was full of mirth.
Through the ages the sun has held our attention,
For various civilisations, it has been the object of celebration.

So in eastern India they perform the "Chhath" festival and never tire,
They congregate, they fast and offer prayers to the ball of fire.
This year at home, it was Geeta's turn to do the honours,
Although in the last 4 score and 8 years - within the Sahay clan -there were no takers.

So family members were informed, who came from far and wide,
The circle of friends made time, to be with Geeta's side.
The house was cleaned and they revamped the pool,
"Prerna's" facade was draped with lights, which shone like a jewel.

There was a buzz in the air and the atmosphere did sizzle,
With so many willing hands, the work was a doddle.
Music was playing and there was a constant chatter,
The whole house was involved and there filtered through tinkling laughter.

Regular food and sweets for the festival were made,
New containers and fruits were bought and on the table displayed.
The whole thing was a 5-day affair,
But the preparation for the "puja" with near and dear ones, made it seem like a spring fair.

Chhath Celebration

Then the evening came when everyone ate "Kheer and Puri",
It was all part of the festivities, which highlighted the sun's glory.
The next day it was time to pay sun, the homage with dedication,
So into the pool went Geeta, with eyes turned up to the source of creation.

People milled around and all offered their prayers,
At the back of their minds, was a genuine desire for everyone's welfare.
While the ritual was enacted, photographs were being snapped,
And soon the people who were not there, were getting these photos
as they were quickly being WhatsApped.

This was the day when they prayed to the setting sun,
The final morning's ceremony was to happen as the next day begun.
This was the moment when the eyes searched for sunrise,
Milk and honey were poured in the water while they all gazed to the skies.

Then it was all over with a sense of joy and a sigh of relief,
As people could scarce imagine, for performing "Chhath"
in the Sahay household was really beyond belief.
Now the deed was done,
Geeta's determination had won.
And so my mum waxes eloquent about how difficult it would be for anyone
in the family for Geeta's grit to emulate,
However that should not detract from the maxim,
that all we ever need to do is to love life and celebrate.

In the pink of health, the newborn's cry does resound,
To the parents their joy knows no bound.
A synthesis of both mum and dad has been sculpted,
Energetic golden thoughts conceived and ambitions constructed.

When the child takes the first tiny step to school,
Joy perfuses their hearts as they witness the sparkle of their jewel.
However trials and tribulations form part of normal life,
There will be times as teenagers, when they will feel blue and be in strife.

School gives way to university and then they knock on the real world,
The purple of life is intriguing but the curtains gradually get unfurled.
At the beginning there is the green of inexperience and youth,
As time marches on they meet envy and vigour on the route.

At work, swings can occur from the red of abashed to the sophisticated black,
Pale handiwork transforms to earthy brown when they bounce back.
When the right blue meets the right pink,
Hearts flutter and soar together in a wink.
Love blossoms in the air, and lends its purple to romance,
Eros leads to Pragma, when after the first glance, they slip into an everlasting passionate trance.

Red intermingled with white, culminates into marital bliss,
Signifying passion sprinkled onto virtue, conjuring memories which would be a delight to reminisce.
The cycle of life is nearly complete, with the next generation's conception,
All the colours of life splashed together in a rainbow, bringing harmony,
by stimulating emotional perception.

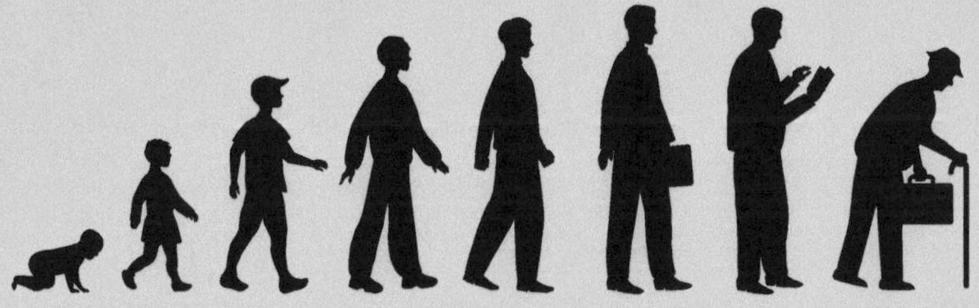

Colours of Life

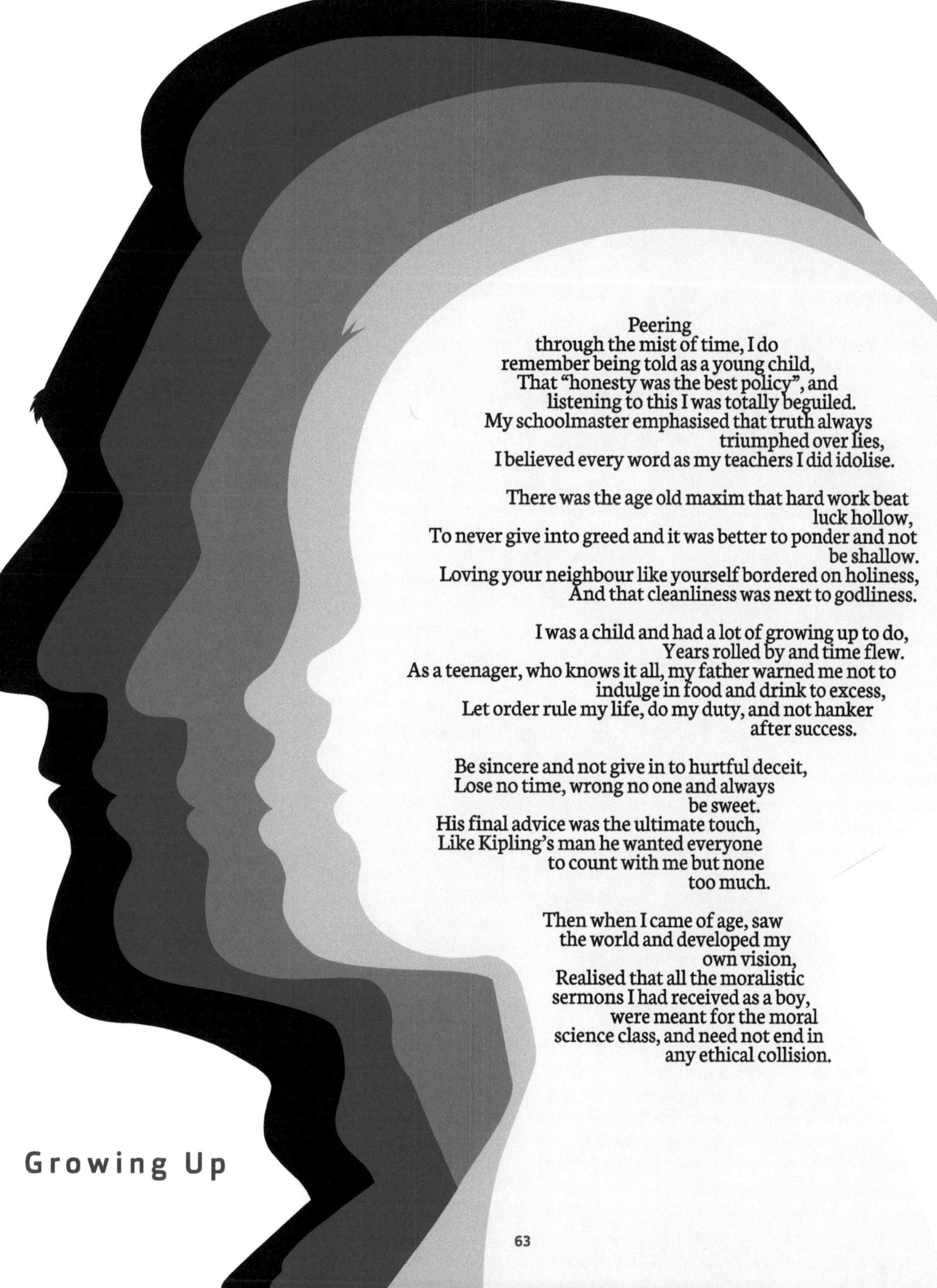

Peering
through the mist of time, I do
remember being told as a young child,
That "honesty was the best policy", and
listening to this I was totally beguiled.
My schoolmaster emphasised that truth always
triumphed over lies,
I believed every word as my teachers I did idolise.

There was the age old maxim that hard work beat
luck hollow,
To never give into greed and it was better to ponder and not
be shallow.
Loving your neighbour like yourself bordered on holiness,
And that cleanliness was next to godliness.

I was a child and had a lot of growing up to do,
Years rolled by and time flew.
As a teenager, who knows it all, my father warned me not to
indulge in food and drink to excess,
Let order rule my life, do my duty, and not hanker
after success.

Be sincere and not give in to hurtful deceit,
Lose no time, wrong no one and always
be sweet.
His final advice was the ultimate touch,
Like Kipling's man he wanted everyone
to count with me but none
too much.

Then when I came of age, saw
the world and developed my
own vision,
Realised that all the moralistic
sermons I had received as a boy,
were meant for the moral
science class, and need not end in
any ethical collision.

Growing Up

As a
young man with a family,
ready to take on the whole world,
I looked at my leaders, whether political, academic
or religious.
And realised that they said one thing, meant something else
and got away even when they did something sacrilegious.

So I became convinced that in essence honesty and truth were
fine as long as it did me suit,
For fooling the taxman was acceptable as it just needed
an accountant astute.
I looked at the mirror and realised that I had finally grown up,
My mind was clear and there was no mix up.

Buddha and Gandhi were eccentrics and were best kept at a
distance on a pedestal,
Otherwise they would ruin the social order and cause
problems incredible.
The "Golden Rule" was empty rhetoric, aimed to impress children,
For the "civilised" adult society was run by "Machiavelli"
although naive humanists considered him a villain.

Now that I am a parent and have children of my own,
I teach them the same claptrap that would
make an adult groan.
I know it is dishonest to tell them
that truth always triumphs,
while we indulge in lies.

But then I also convince them
about the fairies and
Santa Claus,
And only when they grow up will
they realise how hypocritical we are,
And that whatever they had heard as
children were empty words, hiding
life's flaws.

Pulak Sahay

When my father died, I paused and my life just upped and ran,
With colours of emotion splashed across the palette of my soul.
I could peer back down the winding path of where my life began,
And steadily my history unfolded as if watching a movie in an old cinema hall.

I was a young lad, rearing to go,
The orange of vitality seeping out of my every pore.
Down to earth and rustic in my attitude,
Brown in colour and never feeling sore.

There was love in the air and my violet waistcoat exuded elegance,
But when my lady love did not respond.
The mood became blue, the heart saddened,
And the pain was prolonged.

But then peaks follow troughs and after blue comes yellow,
Grief gave way to joy as the lady's hard heart did mellow.
Securing a job and having a family life was next in line,
The red of passion blended into the green of stability and life soon started to shine.

We had been children but now we had our own,
The pure and innocent begetting more of the same bright light.
The indigo of wisdom merging into the serene blue,
And all the colours of the rainbow culminating into white.

Now I am the grandad in the grey of my life,
With my children and grandchildren filling the atmosphere with their tinkling
laughter akin to a gold mine.
Interspersed at times with stress, having the need to make the grade,
Living their lives as I have already lived mine.

Expressions - Rainbow of Emotions

Over two scores of consultant life was brought to a close early on,
Heavy drapes of responsibility removed leading to a new dawn.
Endless possibilities danced on the horizon,
Like the Aurora of life beckoning me on.

It was a repeat performance of thirty years ago,
When I had left the comfort of my parent's twelve-bedroom home.
And ventured abroad with 2 suitcases in hand,
As I did not want to live my life in monochrome.

With no job assured, but a desire to make the grade,
Tears and sweat had made a gritty amalgam then.
Which with perseverance and dedication helped me fight,
All the odds time and again.

Now in my sixties a new chapter was opening up, with myriad possibilities,
To live life in its fullness, no holds barred.
Do all the things one had dreamed of doing,
But been restricted in the past as then the mortgage and school fees were constantly accruing,
Like a millstone around the neck dragging me down and leaving me scarred.

However with retirement on my side the whole world looked bright,
No pressure to leave for work early morning, while it still looked like night.
I could pick and choose what I wanted to do,
Write poetry, do a bit of painting or visit Peru.

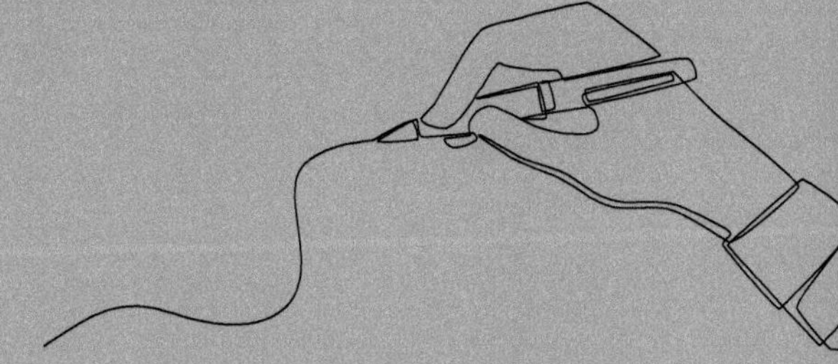

New Beginnings

The children had flown the coop, they were settled in their own life,
I had for company the entire 24 hours of the day and as a bonus, there was also my wife.
So I set about enjoying the remainder of my time,
But for that you needed friends and so I trotted down my memory track,
To begin with I searched and found my school yearbook from 50 years back.

It had the striped cover, the school emblem and faded sepia coloured photos from the past,
I then made contact and rang my friends who then emerged from the shadows at last.
There had been 46 of us in our class, who had bid each other farewell 50 years ago,
each sculpting their own pathway,
Now 5 decades later, we were 7 short and age had withered us,
but the teenage spirit persisted and would remain so till our dying day.

So now we meet in another December 50 years down the line,
To reminisce about our school and exchange memories about things
we had done during that time.
This I am sure will put a spring in our step for the foreseeable future,
Goad us to draw closer,
And do things collectively with an altruistic slant,
And achieve happiness by providing a deserving student with a generous grant.
This will be a new beginning when the golden rays will permeate through the dusk of our lives,
Giving us joy and contentment for as long as we survive.

My birthday was on the 18th of November 1952,
So once a year then, they all sang to me - "Happy Birthday to you".
It then became a ritual that was celebrated on an annual basis,
For me, my birthday was a memorable occasion that left me feeling vivacious.

I was so hooked to it that I felt special during the whole month of November,
I would then step into my birth week,
which finally culminated into the all important special day's splendour.
It would end with the cake cutting and the age old jingle,
With everyone singing "Happy Birthday to you" which into one tune did finally mingle.

Teenage years rolled into adulthood but the set pattern did not change,
Even after I had children of my own, my birthday was still special to me,
though some of my staid friends thought my attitude was a bit strange.

As a young lad I had considered myself immortal, never to decease,
And I always thought that my birthdays would never cease.
But when the black of my hair changed to grey,
It dawned on me that life being finite would finally fade away.

So following retirement my ideas did transform,
As the rising number of candles on my cake reminded me,
of the dwindling balance of my years, leaving me wiser but forlorn.

Time was marching on and this one must never forget,
That each day spent, leaves us a bit deeper in debt.
One day the balance will be wiped out and I will bid the world adieu,
And then, come the 18th of November, no one will ever sing for me,
The beautiful jingle - "Happy Birthday to you".

Birthday

The nights in winter are cold and the pavements wet,
There is little to eat and in the sweltering June heat, you constantly sweat.
On the London Underground platform you busk and keep your arms spread,
but hope gets brushed aside,
As you keep looking at the passersby, with your eyes peeled wide.

The trains stop and the passengers spill out,
They walk, they run, they mill about.
No hesitation, not a glance is cast, while the crowds talk shop,
As for them you don't exist or are just part of the architectural backdrop.

Expectation when not fulfilled is painful,
It is like "Waiting for Godot" and is mournful.
Crouching in the shadows against a pillar, sheltering from the rain,
A cardboard box- your house, and a dog, your only mate, sharing your pain.

Hoping the good people from the food bank, dole out something to eat,
While you try to keep your body and soul together while living life on the side street.
However life passes you by as you are smack in people's blindspot,
They walk around you, keeping a safe distance, avoiding a direct contact,
and never wanting their eyes to be caught.

It is a slur on the sixth largest economy of the world,
If a quarter of a million people on the sidewalk lay curled.
No security, no identity, or a roof over their head,
Lack of emotional wellbeing or a sense of belonging and living in constant dread.

Waiting for people's charity so that they can be fed,
Being considered an eyesore by the public which is why some homeless would prefer to be dead.
Waiting for a scrap of food,
Waiting for a blanket so that the cold it can exclude.
Waiting for a kind word from the public on the road,
Waiting for a fixed abode.

Life for the homeless is misshapen and weakened,
It is the never ending waiting game.
Waiting for people's conscience to be awakened,
So that their shame overpowers them,
leading to actions that on occasions does also lead to incidental fame.

Waiting
Prateeksha

Silence betokens consent- so said Sir Thomas More,
Highlighting the importance of fertile silence and bringing it to the fore.
The noisy workings of the philosopher's mind never does get heard,
Until the splash it makes when in black and white on paper it gets transferred.

There is the attentive silence of the parent, absorbing the turmoil of the teenage child,
Understanding the agitation and helping to pacify,
the mental tsunami, rocking the offspring's mind.
With artistic creativity- silence is the integral ingredient,
that integrates various fragments into a cohesive whole,
Whether it be a painting, poetry, sculpture or a symphony touching the soul.

The silence of apathy is depressing and can lead to lethargy,
lassitude and torpor,
It weighs heavy on the mind,
leading to silent screams that can tear the insides asunder.
But then sitting alone in the sunset,
watching the golden orb take a dip in the ocean,
The silence of awe pervades your being,
stimulating euphoric emotion.

A terrible thing the silence of rejection - a coldness
that can chill your inner core,
Make you feel worthless and unwanted
and shatter you evermore.

Finally it all ends, with the silence of the grave,
In a pit six feet deep and buried under the ground.
Quiet for eternity, be it a king or a knave,
Mingling with the soil and becoming dust,
making a permanent home
where the worms abound.

Silence
Khamoshi

The world wakes up to the crackling of the sunbeams, crimson with desire,
The song of the invisible birds in the treetops above, with shimmering gold
of the sunrise fire.
The rustling of the leaves in the canopy of the oak tree, heaving with content,
The pitter patter of raindrops leaving the clouds,
aiming for the parched earth with abandon and intent.

The incessant hum of the bees, when they pay a visit to the flowers in the garden,
The howl of the husky in the kennel outside, demanding his load be unburdened.
The cooing of the pigeons while they splatter the underneath,
The hooting of the owl, prior to it snatching up its prey beneath.

The chirping of the cricket on a moonlit summer night,
The whoosh of the cool breeze in the evening, fills everyone with delight.
The tinkling of the brook cascading over the rocks,
The swoosh of the rushing wind, that with the majestic trees it talks.

The lapping of the waves on the sands, at the seashore,
The shriek of the seagull, when it dives for fish evermore.
The rumble of the waterfall that froths at the base,
Leading to the rippling of the plunge pool, that finally attains solace.

Following the humdrum of the day, the lotus retires for the night,
The resident frogs in the lily pool, croak to proclaim their birthright.
Far away in the skies, the moon prances amongst the cloud,
The stars wink and twinkle, adding sparkle to the vast nightly shroud.

Nature's sounds are the expression of the divine,
From the depth of the oceans to the mountain tops, it is part of a grand design.
Whether it be a flutter of the butterflies wings or the lion's roar,
The cosmos gives vent to its myriad emotions, leading ultimately to pleasures galore.

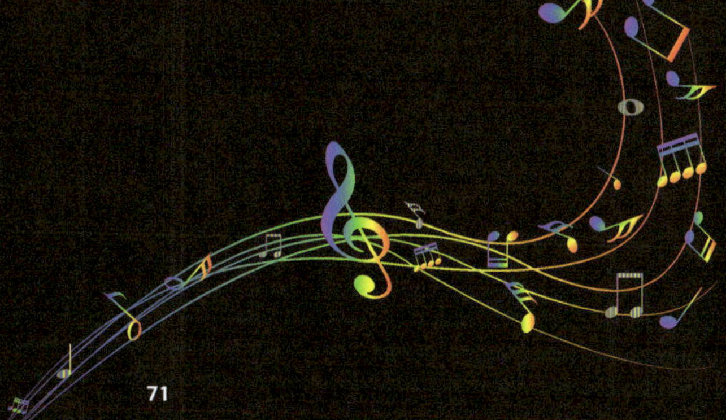

Sounds of Nature

Dictators wield power and monarchs do the same,
But once they are deposed, all they face is shame.
Coercive power, does not last long,
It is only effective, if the leader's position remains strong.

Power of the reward is a matter of give and take,
If the reward is not worth it, then you don't give a toss.
And then as power seeps away,
it shows the common man's strength and the leader's loss.

Legitimate power derives from the standing of the office,
It is the age old story of the chair and its premise.
Once the chair is no more and the office does disappear,
Then with no office and no chair the power vanishes into thin air.

Expert power on the other hand, stands its ground,
And though limited in scope, it is still quite sound.
As it stems from knowledge, acquired by hard work,
Affecting a limited audience who are part of a select network.

Charismatic power is a gift, innate to the person concerned,
There is no logic to it and the leader has it without it being earned.
The personality has an aura which charms the masses,
Power exudes from the leader and in its clutch fall people of all classes.

When there is love for the entire humankind,
Selfless, generous, magnanimous and noble in design,
Stimulating the inner core of people, affording them peace of mind,
Encouraging them to be glad to be enslaved, by the leader whose power is benign.

These are the Gandhi, Mandela, Teresa and Martin Luther King,
Whose persona electrified millions, that led to the public worshipping.
No questions asked, the following was unconditional,
Their supporters would sacrifice themselves, as a matter of principle.

Such power is rare, but is pure and bright,
It never dims but rather with time, achieves greater height.
It encompasses all, even the adversary in the crowd,
Who ultimately succumbs to the love, that envelops them in a compassionate cloud.

Power Shakti

Womanhood is a rainbow of attributes,
Which through the prism of human endeavour, flowers - after taking firm roots.

Red like Radha in love with her Kanha,
The archetypal lover, who surrenders her soul to Krishna,
Merges her identity with that of Sudarshan,
Becoming one in her entirety with Madan Mohan.

Orange is the flavour of Ma Saraswati's brains.
Bringing order where usually chaos reigns,
Exuding warmth while promoting creation and freedom.
Epitome of music, poetry and wisdom.

Yellow embodies Athena - wise and tenacious.
A friend of the brave and ever gracious,
Affords protection to her brood and those in need,
Great administrator and by her actions does lead.

Green is Lakshmi - generosity personified.
With abundance, harmony and prosperity on her side,
Her inner radiant beauty shining bright.
Like the mother divine leading from darkness into light.

Blue is tranquility with mercy as the prime trait.
Protecting all her progeny whatever it takes,
A Buddha in the making, with trust as a dogma she does profess,
Call her by any name, but she is a goddess.

Violet represents Power - the nobility of Shakti.
The fertility, marital bliss and devotion of Parvati,
Durga is invoked to kill demons in their score,
Kali destroying evil and balance does restore.

The varied colours of the spectrum on merging become white.
Representing purity and innocence which can shine bright,
But could also represent a totally blank slate.
On which circumstances can etch histories that could liberate,
Womanhood is a series of waves with a trough and a peak,
Once in unison it leads to achievements unique.

Womanhood

Desolate shopping malls opening on to an empty street,
Venturing to buy food tends to be the only treat.
There are no crowds as moving outdoors for non-essential purposes is banned,
The reason is a total lockdown as per Number 10's command.

If you haven't heard, they say that this is due to the "China Virus" of Donald Trump,
Because of it the world's economy has gone into an eternal slump.
2020 & beyond have borne the brunt of this pandemic leading to sorrows obscene,
But contrary to Trump's ideas the scientists called it Covid-19.

The hospitality sector landscape has turned inhospitable and bleak,
Salons, libraries, cinemas & museums are off the chart.
Business is on hold with incomes drained & unrelenting expenses have havoc wreaked,
Light at the end of the tunnel looks dim with people's lives falling apart.

Stay at home to save lives & protect the NHS is the mantra espoused,
It is a simple message aimed to curb the Covid devastation & has had the masses aroused.
But the sting in the tail is the woman who is the brunt of domestic abuse,
Stuck in the house by law and whose woes are profuse.

Children are the next victims who can't go to school & with their friends their interaction is put on hold,
From poorer families if they come losing out on a meal has an impact adverse.
Can't study from home if laptop numbers are scarce,
Leads to mental, physical and emotional trauma untold.

The hospital wards are full and regular elective work is at a standstill,
ICU is bursting at the seams and patients are dying in their droves.
So to buck up the morale of the eternally tired & washed out nurses and doctors
they have been dubbed heroes,
So though during the first wave they couldn't get provisions as the public indulged in panic buying,
Leading to ITU nurses frustrated and crying,
They got compensated by having the country clapping for them one day a week,
What if they were exhausted and hungry - at least the applause on TV was something unique.

Two million are dead worldwide till date and the count goes on causing untold fright,
But there are some who still profess this to be a conspiracy of the government wanting
to curb individual's right.
Infringing on their freedom using this Covid-19 ploy which they say is just akin to the flu,
Until someone in their family or friend circle dies leading to a lot of wailing and change.
in their angle of view.

Long Lonely Tunnel of Covid

The global purpose of controlling this pandemic is top priority,
The Vedic concept of "Vasudhaiva Kutumbakam"
is the essence driving and goading humanity.
With grit and sweat the timeline of producing the vaccine
has been squeezed and achieved the goal,
What would take years has been done in months
because of the tenacity of mankind's heart and soul.

Immunisation is the only weapon left to vanquish this invisible malevolence,
With this vaccine the world hopes to suppress this
disease and attenuate its prevalence.
The hope being that tomorrow the darkness
and fog of hopelessness will lighten,
And the dawn will not be held back.
The glimmer, with perseverance,
should soon brighten,
And life will be back on track.

The destination was set, while my path had meandered,
On main roads and then scenic routes where occasionally
the potholes led to my journey being hampered.
I thought, being clear minded, my goal was fixed,
But as time elapsed it became evident that my aim in life was a
moving target which led to my emotions being mixed.

As a school boy I wanted to wear collarless coats and snazzy jeans,
Dance the jive and twist and attract the teenage queens.
Have the lead role in the One Act Plays,
Represent my school in elocution contests and set the auditorium ablaze.

On passing out of school my career did loom ahead,
Getting into medical college was everyone's choice.
The competition was tough.
And the going was rough.
But with tenacity and hard work I did succeed, giving the opportunity to my entire family to rejoice.

Medical training is a long haul.
The hours drag on and the emergency duty can make you bawl.
It is not a job but a vocation,
And only when you make the grade can you be the subject of ovation.

Medicine done and a speciality chosen,
Becoming a consultant and in the job have some teaching commitments
interwoven.
Appointed an examiner for the Royal College,
Set question papers for the gastroenterology section,
displaying my knowledge.
There was not a lot more to do as I had already, in my hospital,
set up the services from scratch,
It felt that I had reached the pinnacle of my career
and was the leader of my patch.

My Journey

And then one day it dawned on me that I was of no consequence,
Being just full of sound and fury and would go out with a fizzle,
Here today, gone tomorrow not causing even a ripple.
Cut down to size, I then wanted to reappraise my aims and the route taken,
As the feeling of importance I had felt, I knew, was misplaced and that I had been totally mistaken.

At that very moment when this thought struck me, my path straightened
and the potholes did disappear,
Taking retirement, working for charity and writing poetry turned out
to be a masterstroke and made my mind very clear,

As it left me no time to chase a mirage and consequently wallow in despair.
Add in painting, photography, interacting with friends and family as well
as providing help with child care.

Has gone on to make this last lap of my journey ultimately worthwhile,
And best of all my lips are now adorned by this permanent non-fading smile.

The Lancet was thrust on to the lawyer
Who was given the job of a Sawyer
He knew nothing of this distant land, the people or their culture
But within a month or so, his actions ensured, that these alien people ended up like
carrion in the talons of a vulture.

The jewel in the crown was due to drown,
So a great game was played and India was betrayed.
A squiggly pencil, in an ignorant hand, on an unfamiliar map,
Drew a crooked Line, which dropped India into a heap of scrap.

Divisive politicians spewed venom and fire
While nationalists were unable to conceal their ire.
But the imperialists knew how to divide and rule
And following the midnight hour, the subcontinent's population was thrown asunder, in
an emotional whirlpool.

Brother hacked brother with friendship making a quick exit through the side door
Sisters and mothers were fair game, with animal instinct of humans, reigning supreme,
leaving everyone's heart extremely sore.
Millions were uprooted, they lost their home, their friends, their livelihood, their pride.
In short this was the subcontinent's holocaust, the Indian genocide.

Partition
Batwara

So while the leaders were making a tryst with destiny, awakening at the stroke
of midnight, to freedom and life.
The common man on both sides of the Radcliffe Line was being subjected to
fearsome life changing strife.
Snaking creakingly the human exodus, trudged in opposite directions,
accompanied by a din of sobs and cacophony of heart-rending wail.
So thick hung the pall of dust, that neither Bhagwan nor Allah were able to
peer through the haze and make out the dust-caked faces of the pale and the
limping frail.

Where the Lord failed can his creator be far behind,
Ladling inhumanity was the hallmark of some aristocratic men, whose frame
of mind was rightly maligned.
That nightmare still haunts the Himalaya, down to the Vindhyas and the
Satpura peaks,
Churning the waters of the Sindhu and Ganga up to Kaveri, as from the depths
of their bosom, emanates shrill shrieks.

75 years on, the nation moans and groans, pleading with her children who
have their lesson still not learnt,
She deplores "Bharat ke Tukde" slogans, and beseeches all to come together, to
keep Hindustan a whole, and not to once again, get their fingers burnt.

(First Face to Face SS Baithak at Vaishali's place on 09-10-22 after Covid-19
Lockdown but now to Zoom as going to India to see Mummy)
Baithak postponed as Ramesh Ji (Varsha Ji's husband) passed away.
Rendered at Ranchi, India via Zoom on 18-02-2023

Suspicion in Quotes

Suspicion, says Shakespeare, haunts the guilty mind.
Conflict, as per Hinckley, grows out of ignorance, suspicion and such kind.
Suspicion is the heavy armour, which Burns proclaims, impedes more,
than it protects.
Suspicion is the companion of mean souls, according to Paine,
and the bane of good society, which it affects.

He who is corrupt is naturally suspicious, reiterates Johnson,
and he that becomes suspicious will quickly become corrupt.
Love and suspicion can't dwell together, holds Dumas,
as where the latter enters, the former exits, in a manner abrupt.
Suspicion and jealousy, never did help any man,
in any situation, insists Lincoln, the incorrupt.
Once suspicion is aroused, then Barr says, that everything feeds it.
As suspicion often creates, what it suspects, asserts Lewis,
leading to a gnawing in your stomach pit.

Gordon Hinckley: American Religious leader 20th century | Thomas Paine: English born American founding father | Political philosopher 18th Century | Amelia Barr: British born American Novelist 19th Century | Hosea Ballou: American clergyman 18th Century | Lincoln Chafee: American politician 20th Century

Suspicion is far more wrong, than right , maintains Ballou, more often unjust than just.
So it is better to be occasionally cheated, contends Forbes,
than be perpetually suspicious, and be weighed down by mistrust.
A hundred suspicions, feels Dostoevsky, don't make a proof or give a confirmation.
So Chekhov urges, that you must trust and believe in people,
or life becomes impossible, and can end in perpetual damnation.

He who does not trust enough, mouths Lao Tzu, will not be trusted.
So opines Hemingway, that the best way to find out if you can trust somebody,
is to trust them, which leaves you well adjusted.
Johnson again feels, that it is better to suffer wrong, than to do it,
and happier to be cheated, than not to trust.
As trust is the first step to love, proclaims Premchand with his masterly literary thrust.

Then suspicion goes out of the window & trust is firmly entrenched.
With suspicion in the driving seat, life's bulwark is shaken to the core,
like termites rotting the wood.
So important it is to make a stop to the damage, and engender trust,
which Chafee says, is built with consistency and can once again lead to brotherhood.

A bridge spanning time and space.

A message from the past materialising in the present,
A connection made by actions deliberate, but pleasant.

Thoughts poured in generous proportions into life's bowl,
 and moulded steadily into shape, sans fanfare.
Opening a window, giving a glimpse into the sender's soul,
All strengths and weaknesses exposed - laid totally bare.
No instant gratification but consciously Love's labour nurtured with care,
akin to already beautiful eyes being embellished by kohl.

Waiting for reciprocation,
Tinged with anticipation,
Occasionally with some apprehension.

Such is the letter where emotions dominate,
And emoticons play no role,
Being totally inappropriate.

The plop of the letter on the floor,
When the postman drops it through the door.

The face lights up as the smile reaches the eyes,
and joy is difficult to conceal,
The pulse quickens and warmth spreads all over,
making the recipient feel surreal.

The sender's handwriting,
conjures up a delightful image of zeal,
The stamp with the postmark, leaves a personal appeal.

The address on the letter advertises
the sender's hand with pride,
Giving an invitation to take up the offer to cut open
the envelope and dive inside.

The Letter

Wallow in the depths of all the news and views provided,
And in that instant become one with the sender, merging your thoughts,
leaving nothing divided.

The texture of the paper, on which the letter is wrote,
Takes you back to the stage, when the sender sat at their desk,
and the moment they did devote.
With the feel of the letter you get transported into time,
Experiencing the atmosphere and mood of the person,
which at that juncture would border on the sublime.

It is not only a conversation being had, across what might seem like an
aeon,

And you reliving the experience of their triumphs, without composing a paean.

Letter writing is that art, which helps join hearts with mind,
A place where the two players, get intricately entwined.

Where today social media and instant messaging, are like fast food options,
and all pervasive,
Letter writing is the home cooked full balanced meal, that gives pleasures extensive.

Giving space to creativity, immediacy you discard,
Mindfulness seeps in displacing anxiety, with calmness being in the vanguard.
Concentrating on reflection before thoughts are transcribed,
The paper carries the load of the emotions, which in ink is then described.

This is the letter, a means of conversation, which has come through the ages.
Operative in brightening up someone's day,
and in the case of Washington and Einstein, changing the course of history in stages.

Mum was always here, mum is here no more.
Peering through the mist of time, I can see a caring mother,
In spite of her hectic doctor activity, we children were never a bother.
As a junior doctor, she was always run off her feet,
But whenever the time came to deal with my father, she was so terribly sweet.

I grew up with my nani - her mother - who was a demanding person,
But for mum, it was part of her daily life, and on her mother, she never cast any aspersion.
For patients my mum, was always brimming with compassion,
There were times when her patients were desperately ill,
that I have seen her stop eating, and nearly turn ashen.
This love for people, she spread far and wide,
As a result all her relatives and friends made a beeline for her, as for them she was a goddess personified.

Then as a professor in the medical college, she took her responsibility seriously,
For every lecture she would prepare from the latest books, and teach the students assiduously.
Her juniors loved her and respected her no end,
So when she retired, she was felicitated at a public function,
and presented with a memento that said "Living Legend".

Following retirement my mum lived for over three decades and five,
During this period she lived life to the full, and her zest for life did thrive.
Every morning after showering and getting dressed, she would sit in the living room, gracefully,
Accompanied by her diary and a mobile,
she would embark on making contact with her friends, quite faithfully.

She would not expect a phone call in return,
So even if no one rang her back, she would still call them, and ask after their welfare, showing concern.
This gesture of her's had a great effect, on each one of her contact,
As a result they all reminisced about her phone calls, which had created an untold impact.

So at her funeral, when she had been, shy of a century by five,
It dawned on me that she and her memory, were still vividly alive.

It would be a disservice to her memory, for such a personality as her's, to mourn,
For she was as alive today, as on the day that she was born.
So such person's life, needs to be celebrated, as she always spread good cheer,
Mum is here no more, but mum will always be here.

C e l e b r a t i o n

The book mark in my soul, opens to her satin visage,
The depth of her wistful eyes, conjures up a mirage.
The rustle of her silken hair, cascading over the shoulders, tumbling onto her waist petite,
Fires my desire, which gets lit by the heat from her inner core, thumping my heartbeat.

I hear the music, of her magical gaze,
The breeze from her wafting dress, would have set my soul ablaze.
I see the gleam, of her Cinderella feet,
Leaves creases in my memory, and an ache, which is bittersweet.

Her gentleness soothes my turbulent mind,
Her velvet voice does bandage my heart, which to love is resigned.
The scent of her tinkling laughter, intoxicates me beyond repair,
Leaving me breathless with desire, but the inability to consummate, fills me with despair.

I imagine the red succulent lips, ready to divulge the feelings of her heart,
Dark sultry eyes, goading her smoky voice, which can then her inner secrets impart.
High cheekbones, nudging the eyebrows to arch up proud,
Charm and elegance being her second nature, with a body well endowed.

Lush bodied hair like the enchanted forest, where you can disappear,
Alabaster skin with porcelain face, and a personality full of cheer.
Manicured hands which in her coyness, she uses to hide her face,
An Angel walking on earth, sets your heart fluttering, with her grace.

The inadvertent brush of her dainty hands, would have sent tingles up my spine,
I could hear the violins playing, when her smile caresses her eyes divine.
But she remains unaware, of distress and damage, she has caused all around,
While I savour the perfume of her desire, knowing fully well, that it is not reciprocated,
And for that, in my emptiness, I will forever remain drowned.

Desire

(An ode to Marilyn Monroe, Madhubala, Madhuri Dixit & Juhi Chawla all rolled into one!)

Mothers smell of tenderness combined with a large dollop of comfort and devotion.
Tinged with reassurance and heaps of soothing emotion.
This fragrance relaxes, it is tranquility personified
The scent of your mother takes you on a rollercoaster of joy ride.

The handkerchief of your lover steeped in her fragrance does allure
Draped in what you deem as her haute couture,
The fragrance shimmers, hanging like the Aurora
Does not matter who it belongs to, whether it be a signorina or a señora.

Coming home to India during the rains, is a treat beyond compare
The musky freshness called petrichor, rises high up in the air,
The pitter patter of rain lands in the crevices of the roads and stoneware
The percussion of raindrops generates a medley of sounds and also a fragrance quite rare,
This scent triggers emotions of homecoming,
bordering on patriotism, which is fine
but should not become nationalism, which can be unbecoming.

Aroma of foods from yesteryears holds a special place
Can be tied up with memories galore of your birth place,
Linked to family and friends and time spent in cracking a gag
Sometimes innocent, other times enjoyable and on occasions can be a bit of a drag.

Then there are parties where perfumes run riot and can seriously abut
Wafting from corner to corner leaving nothing to chance and never be clear cut.
Can be subtle on one end and on the other can overpower all your sense,
You can be bowled over to begin with as fragrances can be intense.

Mother's scent is a pillar of comfort
Lover's aroma does allure,
Fragrance of foods from home evokes memories galore
Fragrance of rain soaked soil can alleviate stress,
Welling up tears of joy.
Perfumes worn by friends alters the mood which one does enjoy,
Fragrance is that essence in the air which can be evasive,
It is spelt desire, tranquility and emotion and this ethereal mix is all pervasive.

Fragrance is Pervasive

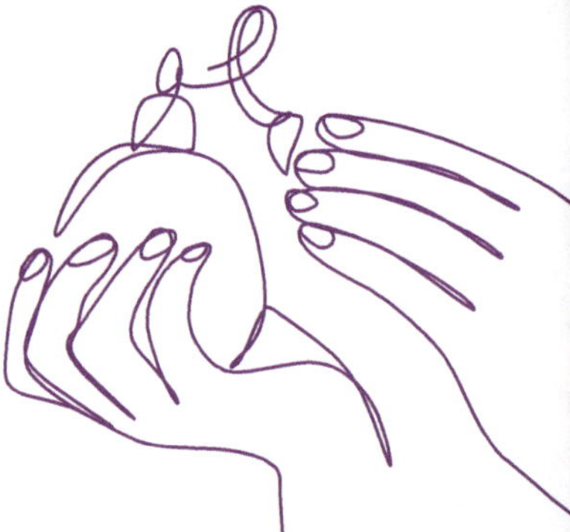

I ask myself whether I am a religious bigot,
And then I confess, that I really am not too sure.
It makes my psyche feel bruised.
Taken up by Hindutva, as I was born in a family of Hindu theist,
Enamoured by the saffron wave,
Happy for the Ram Mandir, but in the process get abused,
By liberals and secularists.
But how is all that even possible, as I profess to be an atheist.
I am so confused.

Antagonised by women clad in burqa and girls wearing hijab,
Upset by the bearded folk, cluttering up the streets on Friday, offering namaz.
I know they do it consciously, as that is how, all the attention they do grab.
But when it comes to Sikhs sporting their turban, I don't mind,
Or the Christians flaunting their cross to all humankind,
And the Jews in their skullcaps being one of a kind.
So why is the Muslim the subject of my ire?
Am I a hypocrite?
I really am not sure.
As all my arguments backfire,
for they at the best of times, seem obscure.
And if the situation were not so serious, I would be bemused
I am so confused.

Is it because Al-Qaeda or ISIS brutalise humanity in the name of Islam.
I know that all Muslims are not terrorists, but then virtually all terrorists today are Muslims.
Still the rest of the Muslim world tries to justify their actions,
And on that basis, they potray being the injured factions.
Is it also because they subjugate the minorities, in which ever country they predominate,
But then clamour for extraordinary rights, when present in smaller numbers,
As what they are aiming for is being part of an Islamic Caliphate.
Is it because for them their religion comes first, across Continents, and the Nation they live in,
matters afterwards, if at all.
Don't know what to think, as this very thought does appall,
The irony is that I feel abused,
I am so confused.

I Am So Confused

I do consider myself secular at heart, and a liberal.
But then does secular in the Indian context mean anti-Hindu
and does a liberal have to be pro-Muslim?
I am not even religious.
As I said earlier, I am an atheist.
Or rather not being brave enough, I would err on the side of being an agnostic,
Which means to say, when it comes to the Almighty,
my arguments tend to be flawed,
Or you could say that I am not gutsy enough to come out of the closet
and declare my non-belief in God.
Am I a coward?
Probably am, and as a result, I do feel disempowered.
Which is why I feel my mind is lost and unused,
I am so confused.

I am an avid student of cosmology,
Believe in evolution and am fascinated by atheism,
Love to listen to Javed Akhtar and respect Richard Dawkins' rationalism.
But still don't have the courage to say-NONE- in the section-religious belief-when
filling up a personal statement form.
But I do want the uniform civil code to be the norm.
I would rather go for "Jhatka" and not eat halal meat,
But then I really don't care what I eat.
Is it because Muslim fanatics want to have their cake and eat it too,
Are there lessons from history that prove a point or two.
Jinnah vivisected India arguing that Muslims and Hindus were two nations
who could never live together
But today in India, there live 200 million Muslims, while their leaders proclaim that they
and the Hindus aren't birds of the same feather,
Post partition all Hindus got straitjacketed into their Civil law, while the Muslim men got
special protection regarding their Islamic views.
Inequality is thus enshrined in the Indian constitution and this does bruise,
Why this step motherly treatment to the Hindus?
I am so confused.

So should we do away with religion completely,
Have one universal civil law for all,
With religion playing no part in public life,
as that is the cause of people's downfall.
Let religion be closeted in the homes at best, and remain a private affair,
No state funding or flaunting on the streets, and no fanfare.
No blaring of "Bhajans" or "Azaan" on loud speakers.
But the problem is that then, the faithful might be up in arms,
with the usual clarion call given, that Islam is under attack.
The politicians would then join in, as they would not want to lose
their trump card during elections, and their chances of a comeback.
With each politician outdoing the other in mollycoddling
the minorities to secure their vote bank,
We would all have gone full circle and still drawn a blank.
So I am at a loss and don't know what to do or think
For if I affirm, to what I have already thought aloud,
then I will as a racist be accused,
As a result I remain muddled, and am so totally confused.

When I ponder about the yonder, seven decades pass in just a flash,
It was only yesterday when at school with friends,
I would be dancing in the common room, with panache.
Those, I think, were the best years of my life, as material gains we did not want to accrue,
But then memories when distant, have the character of, always, acquiring a golden hue.

Memories come in snippets, discreet bundles and not a continuous flow,
More like still photographs, as opposed to a movie or a floor show.
There was the darkroom, where I learned the photographic art,
The stage in the auditorium, where I practised my elocution piece or rehearsed the drama part.
The swimming pool where I honed my aquatic skills,
The tennis court where winning a match, gave me immense thrills.

Life was one merry-go-round and the music never stopped,
Then came college and the fun and games had to be dropped.
Career loomed large with exams being an integral part,
Relaxed attitude had to give away
and I had to start working long and smart.

At some point in time Love tripped me,
By the time I found my feet, I was a father of three.
It was a new country when I got my bearings correct,
Apart from creating a space for myself, the children also learnt to earn their self-respect.
Those memories leave a cuddly feeling and although the picture is a blur,
Old friends came and some friends left, but friendship never did wear a slur.

Children grew up and as expected did fly the coop,
But then new friends appeared and hence our spirits never did droop.
When children leave, can grandchildren be far behind,
So the incessant taxying of children was interrupted by only a brief respite,
before the scurrying after the grandchildren, did border on me losing my peace of mind.

Memories

The beautiful memory, these days, that usually wakes me late in the morning,
Is of sauntering to my study with a coffee, instead of dashing to the hospital,
when called without a warning.
Photography tours beckon me and writing poetry and painting remain a passion,
Contrast it to the time when rushing to the hospital in the middle of the night, did leave me ashen.

Memories are a great prop, a standard against which everything is weighed,
Which is why my memories of my doctor facet, makes my post retirement life feel wonderful,
as I so value my non-medical accolade.
So although my joints creak now, and I walk terribly slow,
The memory of my rallies on the tennis court and the swimming relay race,
always leaves me with a warm afterglow.

On a cold November day 68 years ago,
an ordinary couple were engulfed by an extraordinary glow.
They were expecting their first child,
A boy came in to their world making their joy totally wild.
And they named him Pulak.

Pulak means happiness and the name was apt,
As it brought bliss into my parents lives to which they did beautifully adapt.
But so it would be, whatever the name.
But I still think it was a name well chosen, as it is an unusual one,
as do all my relatives and friends constantly exclaim.

But being unusual has its own drawback,
Once as an 8 year old I went to my school vice principal to get my swimming card,
Which he made out to "Bullock" and not Pulak,
And that name stuck to me for a whole year and which I found difficult to discard.

I also remember my Hindi teacher who in light vein,
Called me "Palak ka Saag" when taking the class attendance,
inspite of keeping a straight face and decorum trying to maintain.

Born in Patna the capital of Bihar my close friends called me "Pulakwa",
For Biharis the suffix "wa" is a term of affection,
Whenever "wa" is added on it engenders a close connection.

Having an unusual name I had virtually no need for a surname,
For I remember friends whose names were so common that they could only be
differentiated by the village they came from,
Or the department of their fathers work which they had to specifically proclaim.
They were the Kurselas and the Bihtas as well as the Electric and Police,
Not so me, for I was the only Pulak there had ever been in my school,
and was a single piece.

But that did not make me any special or top class,
It was as good as, what my American jesuit principal, Father Murphy said,
Francis Kumar Ahmed or Gobardhan Das.

My nickname is Pappu and it is still used by my close family and friends,
Many of them call me Pappu bhaiya,
Bhaiya being elder brother and I like it no end.
But recently there has appeared a sting in the tail,
As the Gandhi family heir in India is known as Pappu
And is a butt of all kinds of jokes and at whose expense the public does regale.
This is something which is difficult to live down,
Which is why I try to stick to my proper name of Pulak so that I don't get branded a
clown.

My Name

In school my surname was Sinha after my best friend,
although my parents were Sahay,
But when it came to my final year I decided to change it by and by.
The reason was quite idealistic.
I detested the caste system and so did not want to be classified
as belonging to a particular caste,
and so became Pulak Kumar.
This being a nondescript surname it helped me bid,
I thought, casteism au revoir.
But life had a lesson in store for me as ground realities tend to be bizarre.

I went to a medical school where my mother happened to be a professor of gynaecology,
So ultimately everyone knew what caste I belonged to and taking cue from my mother's surname,
started calling me Sahay without even a hint of an apology.

It became so entrenched that I lost my idealistic battle and so by a court order
I got my name finally changed,
So for the last 42 years the name Pulak Sahay has been unchanged.
Although whenever anyone asks me my name, I mention Doctor Pulak Sahay,
As I think that inherently I am proud of being a doctor, like all Indians are,
And to a lot of my junior colleagues, nurses and students I still remain
Dr. Sahay, who is a bit of a star.

And I must confess that I quite like it when they do adulate,
Must be that Ego of mine that I have still not been able
to subjugate.
In spite of talking big and of proclaiming that I am of
no consequence,
Somewhere in my subconscious Pulak continues
to hanker after prominence.
But the bottom line regarding my name,
I would want to claim,
Is that whoever comes in touch with me,
I hope, has joy and cheer set aflame.

Absolute belief in truth is mankind's slickest concoction,
Which is why Socrates opted to drink the hemlock potion.
Bandying about the greatness of truth, is for show, and holds no sway,
It is like the elephant's teeth,
The gorgeous outer ones for pomp and show, while the unsightly ones inside, grinds away.

Parents tell their children that honesty is the best policy,
But when it comes to them, the version of their truth becomes more like fallacy.
In public the importance of truth is flaunted and they all wax eloquent,
But actually lies get dressed up as fact, and the one who speaks the truth,
is branded as naive and ignorant.

Politicians swear by the truth and each one is holier than thou,
But when it comes to the crunch, truth is brushed under the carpet
till journalists force them to avow.
Journalists however are no better, as for them, on the altar
of sensationalism, truth they can eschew,
It can all be manipulated, depending on which end
of the rainbow's colour is their political hue-
Whether it is red or blue.

Law and order in certain countries are neither just nor orderly and is usually spurned,
It is tailored to the bank balance and the power of the individual concerned.
Slogans of truth and honesty are plastered on the wall,
That is where they remain permanently to be seen,
while the undercurrent of corruption sweeps away all modicums of rightness, like a flimsy
canoe over a giant waterfall.

Religion is no exception, where their leaders claim direct access to the Almighty,
whether you call him Allah, Bhagwan, The Holy Spirit or the Son,
Ensuring that their version of the truth is fed to the masses so that their will is done.
In the name of religion, loudly proclaimed truths, are accompanied by bloody swords
and shields shining bright,
While believers of other religions are put to death with helpless woman
and innocent children left in a piteous plight.

Truth is usually misused as a guise, a facade wrapped in a cloak and fitted with a mask,
An impersonator at best and looked at as an impostor,
that is employed for people's nefarious task.
Even the ethnic cleanser professes, that truth is on his side,
People are slaughtered in droves but they justify their misdemeanours calmly,
taking it all in their stride.

Truth is a concept best described in philosophical books,
Usually put on a pedestal, out of reach of the
common man and is definitely not for crooks.
Only once in a millenia there comes
a Buddha, a Gandhi, Nanak or Kabir,
Whose entire being and soul does regularly to truth adhere.

But for the rest,
Truth seems to be more a rare exception rather than the rule,
With lies and falsehoods being the order of the day,
establishing its hold on all and sundry which no doubt is cruel.

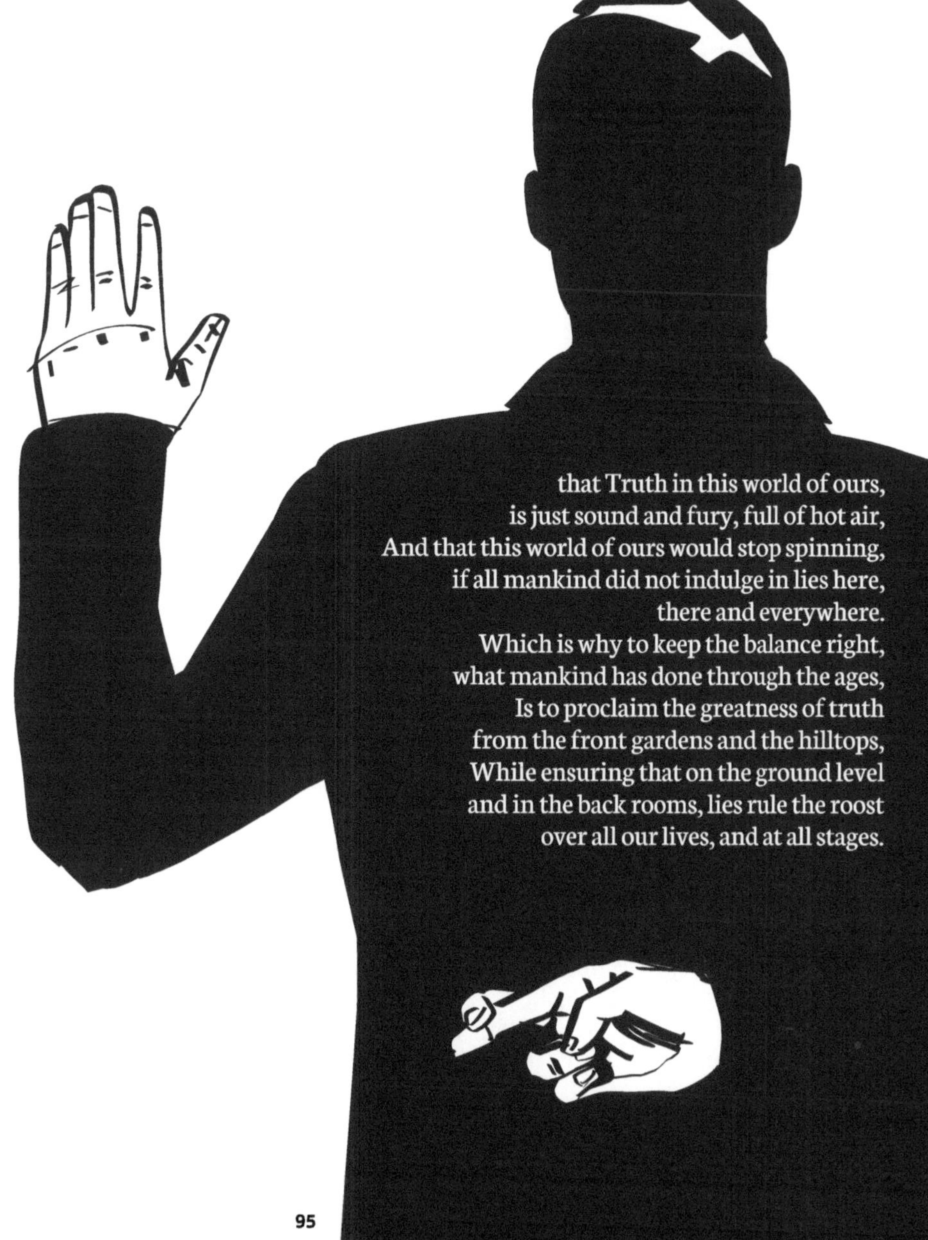

It was the Hundred Years' War
And who made their mark,
A nineteen year old girl nicknamed "The Maid of Orleans"
Who to the wider world became famous as "Joan of Arc".

Five thousand miles away and five centuries later
Appeared on an Indian battlefield another liberator,
Part of the Sepoy Mutiny or was it the Indian rebellion
Depended on which side of the fence you sat on
Whether you were an Indian patriot
Or an imperialist who possessed an advanced weapon.

In the twentieth century, woman have come to the fore
There was the "Lady with the Lamp" who during the Crimean War,
Spread goodwill and cheer amongst the wounded and dying
Looked after the sick and consoled the crying.

While the Polish French woman won Nobel Prizes wholesale
Set up mobile X-ray units on the battlefield on a large scale,
Conducted studies for the treatment of tumours using radioactive isotope
For the forlorn her work stood out as a beacon of hope.

For the deaf and blind there was Keller the torchbearer
Who as a child had been unruly and wild and been a holy terror,
But enter Anne Sullivan and "water" was the first word that made the connection
And this tantrumprone child transformed into a champion of women's suffrage
Espousing socialism to perfection.

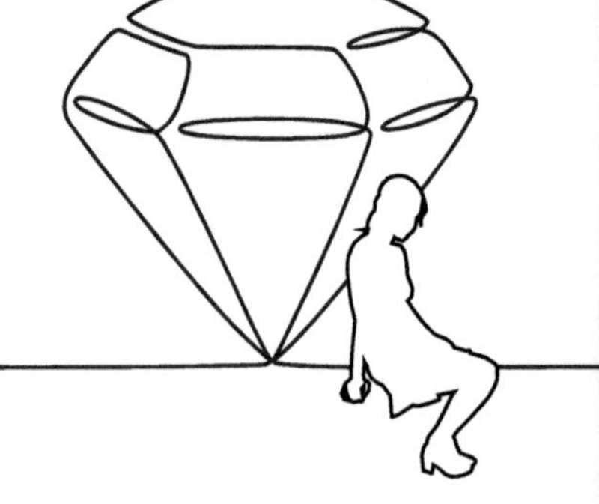

Woman - The Multifaceted Gem

The Civil Rights activist who in the "Montgomery Bus Boycott" played a pivotal role
Was Rosa Parks for whom human rights for all was the only goal,
Fighting against injustice and racial segregation
Was the bedrock on which lay her entire life's Works foundation.

Enter the apostle of love
Who was a gift from Kosovo to Kolkata slums,
She served the least of her brethren with no fanfare or banging of drums
Wedded to chastity and poverty giving free service to the poor
Mother Teresa was the lover of the downtrodden - the archetypal doer.

From physicist to chemist, freedom fighter and civil rights promoter
Women have pervaded through the ages and ultimately ensured that they also became a voter.
Caring for the sick and loving the destitute and the dying
Has seen the fair sex do it all which is ever so gratifying.
Whether it be a disability afflicting the body or the core of the soul
Or a young woman with her infant strapped to her back fighting for her freedom as her only goal.

Women through turmoil have always been a godsend
Getting conjured into becoming super beings
By putting a sprinkling of Saraswati, a dash of Durga and a little Lakshmi into the blend.
That is the reason why women are Nature's diadem
Which is why Pulak considers them each "the multifaceted gem".

Attachment leads to expectations and expectations lead to suffering,
Needing nothing attracts everything.
Connection makes you powerful, while attachment drains the life out of you.
Living in the present ensures, that peace descends on you.

No amount of time is enough for pleasure,
So try not to plot, to make it last forever.
With the best will and all your efforts, it won't.
Hankering after tomorrow-the advice is, that you don't.
Live for the moment even when the going is rough,
With the belief that what you have now, is enough.

Believe in yourself whether anyone else does or not,
Be your own best friend and foster your own thought.
Don't hinge on to anyone or anything, as you are not someone else's other half,
You are separate and another whole, and not any riffraff.
Hold on lightly and not too tight, for it may lead to a sad fate,
Squeezing too tightly can make, both of you suffocate.

Don't dwell in the past for it will never change,
Use yesterdays for lessons learned, and try your memories to rearrange.
Stay open to new connections, always keep an open mind,
Obsessing about tomorrow, wastes life,
As there is always another tomorrow, not far behind.
So live full today,
And don't dwell on yesterday.

Do what you wish now, whatever you love - Don't wait,
No moment is worthier of joy than now, because that is all that will ever fall in your plate.
Pain is inevitable, but suffering is not,
And if a dark moment arrives- don't brood a lot.
Yield to peace and happiness consciously, without a vexing thought.
But don't get carried away, as that too will elapse.
All moments will ultimately pass.
As life is cyclical for all, from the plebeian to the ruling class.

Let It Go
Solution to Aasakti / Attachment

Everything that has a beginning, also has an ending,
All meetings culminate in parting.
Have no fear, remain calm,
Love people in such a way that they feel free, and reciprocate without any qualm.
Never be shaken by praise or blame,
Test everything on the anvil of reason, without any shame,
You can own things but never let them own you, and never get into a huff.
You can depend on people but never be dependant, ensuring your soul remains tough,
Appreciate and enjoy what you have now, for that is always enough.

We don't own anything as we can be dispossessed of them, before long,
Only thing ours is our lives and that too, not for long.
So why the attachment and what for the pride,
Live one day at a time, as that is all you will ever get, before your life is finally denied.

I have an old suitcase, a weather-beaten one,
Frayed at the edges, with scratch marks all over,
but which has given me good service, in the long run.
Not too smart, not shiny at all, but comfortable to hold,
That harbours all my memories - happy, sad, recent and old.

Stuck there in one corner is my childhood, where minor things, did me enthral,
Playing hours on the verandah, on my own, there was still there, my rubber ball.
Imagining seriously what it would be like, to mimic birds in flight,
And then when my pilot uncle took me up for a ride, into the skies,
having the feeling of exhilaration, tinged with fright.

Also under the layer of clothes, I would keep a note, of One Rupee,
A princely sum for a twelve year old, it made me feel gutsy.
I would use it, to treat myself to a milky bar ice cream,
This for me was luxury at its best, that would always make my eyes gleam.

Kept to one side in the same suitcase, were my written accolades and drama prize,
Something that I am so proud of, that it still brings tears of joy, to my eyes.
It gave me inner happiness, and a sense of worth,
And the best part was recognition amongst friends,
whose camaraderie helped me, remain, down to earth.

Placed in the middle, kept nicely folded, were the letters I had wrote,
Professing undying love as a teenager does, and promising that my life to her, I would devote.
However reality checks in, and back to earth you descend,
Exams, teachers and parents loom large in front of you, and soon you forget your lady friend.

In the top pocket of the suitcase, neatly kept, were my travel documents and passport,
And all my medical degrees and certificates, as I had, to the hospital manager, to report.
The apprehension those memories generated, were one of a kind,
As I was all alone in an alien land, with India left far behind.
Kept right on top was my Royal college degree,
Once I had that under my belt, life became stressfree.

Suitcase
Sandook

But then sadness enveloped me as I found under all the clothes, my parents' photo,
As I had lost both my parents, it left me, with a feeling of sorrow.
But then I realised that they had achieved, so much in life, worthy of adoration,
So my thoughts are now transformed, and so whenever I think of them,
it is painted with colours of celebration.

The final item that has been placed, into my suitcase, right at the very end,
Is my pension document, which gives me, loads of free time to spend.
Now that my suitcase has nearly filled up, there is space only for my camera, books and painting kit,
As all my time is dedicated to me, my wife, my friends, and a very occasional babysit.

People might think that I am self-obsessed, as I only think about my happiness, and to be dry-eyed,
But then what is wrong with that, as ultimately everyone just wants to be happy and content,
I am so, and like my suitcase, which has its scratches and its dent,
I have had my share of knocks, but I feel fulfilled and satisfied,
And like my suitcase, I still am able to hold everything together,
and offer support to whoever needs it, all in my stride.

Time is artificial,
it is make-believe.
And hence life without time, would be beneficial,
For you don't need time to live, which anyway is brief.

It is a creation of the human mind,
For the rest of nature, it is of no consequence, and in fact it can be a bit of a bind.
Animals live and thrive, without resorting to time.

The universe began at the Big Bang,
But why do you need to time it, or quantify,
It would still be the Big Bang, whenever it happened,
although we do know that initially things went awry.

A child becomes an adolescent, and then an adult,
Wrinkles appear when you age, and your skin is subjected to insult,
No need to chart out this entire process.
Why to involve time into the equation, and cause more stress.

The Aurora dances in the Arctic night sky,
Time does not make it appear.
The thunder claps and lightening can strike, without the help of time austere.

Tsunamis attack and earthquakes crack,
For which time is not essential.
Butterflies flutter, rainbows adorn, heat swelters and rains can be torrential.
Winds blow, leaves rustle, oceans roar and waves crash,
Flowers bloom, bees buzz, glaciers melt and volcanoes spew ash.
All sans time.

So if you didn't bother about time, there would be no tension,
Like a free bird you would roam the skies, without apprehension.
A tiger in the jungle, ruling the wild,
The dolphin riding the waves as a monarch, self-styled.
No constraint of time, like nature in its rawest form,
Become a yogi and into a Buddha transform.

Time
Samay

Pulak Sahay

The sun was high in the sky,
Been up from dawn, without batting an eye.
Spreading warmth, and glow across the heavens,
Nurturing life on the land, and in the oceans.

But its daily duty was coming to a close,
Soon it would be time for its nightly repose.
But there was still time before the bees slowed down,
And the flitting butterflies retired, from the flowery playground.
The golden yellow tinged, with red and orange bouquet,
Announced that, evening will shortly be on its way.

The clouds settle, the winds slow down,
The lapping waves surround the rocks all around.
The sun takes rest, in between the mountain peaks,
A Crimson hue seeps through, simulating the blush on a bride's cheeks.
The paint across the sky gets dark and grey,
With the demise of light, evening will soon be on its way.

Dusk wraps a cloak of purple, over a sandy landscape,
With slivers of sunlight, breaking through, in a streaky shape.
The crickets take their cue, from the dimming of the sun,
The seagulls mew, as they don't want to be out done.
Then when the red globe gets doused, by the blue sea,
Evening makes an appearance, in a manner carefree.

With the light fading, the celestial sphere, gets splashed by a rainbow,
The air freshens, affording a sweet afterglow.
The stars appear and beckon all, by a wink and a twinkle,
Peace and tranquility descends, affording joy that is liberally sprinkled.
With a kaleidoscope of the city lights, the mind dances, spreading plenty of cheer,
With the sun gone down, and the moon and the stars on the ascent, it is evident that, evening is here.

Evening is Here
Sandhya

Victory's Defeat
Jeet ki Haar

The colossus of Indian politics had attempted, that his promises be fulfilled,
Thousands of kilometres of highways and infrastructure,
across the country were built.
Lofty pledges in the manifesto, that had been made,
Were delivered to the public, properly packaged and shaped.

Swachh Bharat, welfare and health insurance schemes, toilets,
tap water and electricity, to the poor were disbursed,
Direct payments into the have-nots' bank account,
and number of digital payments were in the world, a real first.
Nationalism, security and Chandrayaan were launched,
while India's economy soared ahead,
Abrogation of article 370, Triple Talaq and building the Ram temple,
the BJP thought, would leave the opposition in shred.

So when the time came for the 18th Lok Sabha elections - Modi Ji's third,
The big man thought it was a done deal, and humility got blurred.
The slogan of "400 Paar" was the war cry,
Patting his chest was something, the voters did decry.
Overconfidence, with poor choice of turncoat politicians, caused havoc, in the UP arena,
Announcing from the dais, the irrelevance of the RSS, for the success of BJP,
led to the loss of its patina.

Coupled with anti-incumbency, hubris ruined the day,
Failing to take on board, rural distress, unemployment, paper leaks and Agniveer,
the psephologists were led astray.
Breaking up opposition parties in Maharashtra, lost them, the sympathy of the electorate,
Following the farmers protest, in Punjab, winning seats, was like climbing the Everest.

There was however a silver lining, with wins in Odisha, MP, Delhi, with inroads in the south,
And although with pre poll alliance, BJP has formed a government,
its existence will remain hand to mouth.
The reason for this, was a short supply of modesty,
and lowering one's stance to the level of the opposition,
Baiting the muslims, who then voted en bloc,
to defeat the BJP, being their only ambition.

It is true that the Hindus, have as yet, not coalesced, into one tight knit group,
That caste is still the poison, permeating the Hindu society, causing it to stoop.
But the slur that remains, is the election,
of the villains of Sandeshkhali and secessionists of Punjab,
As well as the hate speech mongers, who are the worst kind of scab.

Now that it is a coalition government, there should be a period of consultative politics,
With federalism ruling the roost, and decentralisation going into the mix.
No place for arrogance, with bravado taking a back seat,
And that, if sincerity holds fast, it just might lead in 2029,
to a repeat of the 2019 feat.

Others:
(Nature's Symphony, Sadness, Happiness, Thinking of You, Peaks and Troughs, How Much Do I love You, The Seasons, Soulmate, Life, Love, The Rains, Thoughts, Words and Deeds, Love Lost, Anticipation, Colours of Nature, Life History of Raindrops, Dawn and Dusk, Globe of Fire, Jewels in the Sky, I Am So Lucky, Icy Winter, Tears, Colours of Life, Growing Up, Expressions- Rainbow of Emotions, New Beginnings, Silence *(Khamoshi)*, Sounds of Nature, Power *(Shakti)*, Womanhood, The Letter, Celebration, Desire, Fragrance is Pervasive, Memories , Woman - The Multifaceted Gem)

Inspirations

The original title of this poem was "Questions and Answers". But then when a school friend of mine, Anwar Jafri, read my poem, he suggested the title "Unanswered Questions" instead. I thought that this title was more apt and hence I changed it.

UNANSWERED QUESTIONS

Driving back from work, the greenery all around, stimulated me. Then while sitting in my bedroom, while I was in a pensive mood, I looked out of the window and there was an expanse of green that was spread in front. This triggered something inside me and I wrote a poem on the colour green, and all that it represented.

THE COLOUR GREEN

My pain was triggered by the scenes of lawlessness and carnage, that I witnessed, while visiting Srinagar on way to Amaranth in 2008. Srinagar at that time was literally and figuratively burning. It so disturbed me that I penned my thoughts and emotions down, soon after I reached my parents' hometown of Ranchi, in Jharkhand.

INDIA'S TRAGEDY

We had gone on an expedition to Antarctica. It was the holiday of a lifetime. The experience was out of this world. It was magical. So after I returned home, I put my thoughts about this trip on paper, and the poem was born.

THE WHITE KINGDOM

This was the first grandchild in our family. So it was a very special occasion. To celebrate Eila's first birthday, I wrote this poem, summing up all our emotions.

EILA ANAMSA

this poem on her, and also reflected upon myself, as ageing is relentless, and does not spare anyone.

MY MOTHER

This poem saw the light of day, following the stunning victory of Mr. Narendra Modi, at the 16th Lok Sabha elections in May 2014. This man was a beacon of hope for millions. Here was a son of the soil, who trounced the first family of India, whose claim to fame had become, nepotism, corruption and dynastic rule. Through this poem I briefly outlined the entire political history of Independent India, as well.

INDIA WINS FREEDOM AGAIN

This reminded me of the sharp, incisive intellect of the common Indian electorate. They were so smart and perceptive, that they consciously dumped Mr. Narendra Modi, within a year of giving him a thumping mandate. They discarded him in favour of the Aam Aadmi Party. It showed the discerning nature of the Indian voter, and filled me with admiration, for the lay Indian public. They proved that the public could never be taken for granted.

THE INDIAN PUBLIC

I remember my father as a smart, dashing, handsome man, when in his prime. For me there was nothing he could not do. But then as age advanced, he became physically frail, although his intellect remain intact. Before his end came, he had become wheelchair bound, which was traumatic for me. And hence I shut his incapacity out, and only remembered him as a dapper young man, with a sharp wit. This helped keep the vision of my father, rosy as ever for me.

PAPA AND THE SEASONS

This was basically my story, although seen through the prism of all overseas Indians or NRI as we are called. It sums up all the trials and tribulations, I went through and all the heartaches, as I tried to return to India, to serve my country, after having my training abroad, but failed. And so here I was, like so many others, trying to contribute my mite, to my motherland, but from far.

PRAVASI BHARATIYA

This is such a painful topic. It touches the core of my heart. Everyone has their own take on it. But there is one common thread, that runs through everybody's mind. That is to stop the illegal migrants. However no one is wanting to take the impossible step to improve the conditions of their home / country to such an extent, that the urge
to migrate illegally is curbed. And hence I wrote this poem, giving vent to my inner feelings.

MIGRANT CRISIS

This in a nutshell is my life story and it highlights my life's philosophy, which I have stuck to and which has paid me rich dividends, as it has opened up the fountains of happiness for me, giving me contentment.

AUTUMN

My wife, Geeta, had decided to participate in this auspicious festival called Chhath. Something that nobody in our family had ever undertaken. So there was a challenge and excitement and apprehension together with the cooperation offered by the extended family to make it a success, which it was. Once the deed was done, there was a perceptible sense of achievement. And so as a true historian, I documented everything for posterity in verse.

CHHATH CELEBRATION

My birthday has always been a very special occasion for me, since I can remember. And contrary to what my peers say, with advancing years, the importance of my birthday for me, has never diminished. Even now it is as important to me, as when my parents celebrated it, when I was a young lad. I always wait excitely, for my friends and family to wish me on my birthday. But then it dawned on me, that one day, when I am gone, no one will wish me a happy birthday, and that my all important birthday will not be of any importance at all.

BIRTHDAY

This was inspired by watching the homeless, sitting outside the superstores, begging. It was a painful experience, watching grownups in a rich developed country, which over a century ago, boasted of having the sun never set over its empire, sitting outside in the cold, waiting for handouts.

WAITING

The Covid pandemic was a life changer for everyone. But it affected me more so as being a doctor, I was in the thick of it. I was a witness to the dread it caused and the heartbreaks as people lost not only their kith and kin but also their livelihood. But then it also showed how the human spirit triumphed over this mammoth adversity and how the whole world got together to fight and curb this disease by mass immunisation. A testament to the human race who can overcome any calamity, if they put their mind to it.

LONG LONELY TUNNEL OF COVID

A snapshot of my life and my thought process that evolved, from having a sense of self importance to realising that in the larger scheme of things, I was of no consequence. And how this realisation, has opened for me, all the doors to happiness.

MY JOURNEY

This was a very emotive topic. Capturing what I call the "Indian genocide" or the subcontinent's holocaust, was heart wrenching. I also realised that there had been no memorial to it for 70 years, which is ever so shameful. We as a nation did not, for such a long time, did anything to remember or honour our dead.However in 2017, the first memorial / museum to "partition" was opened in Amritsar, India.
My poem tends to describe the conditions that led to the Partition, it's horrendous effects and how we must learn from it and not give in to anti national demands of further balkanisation of India.

PARTITION

This was a new technique I tried. The poem that I wrote was constructed, using the quotations of eminent personalities, from across the globe.

SUSPICION (IN QUOTES)

The concept of secularism as flaunted by the "secular liberals" in India, continues for me to be a contradiction in terms. And so with this poem, I have tried to grapple with my own biases, and those of others.

I AM SO CONFUSED

This poem which I wrote in 2020, has been a unique experience, as my name had changed and evolved over the years. Starting as a schoolboy, to the time when I became a doctor. It was not only a paper exercise, but reflected my life, which I had lived through various times.

MY NAME

Looking around me, watching television and listening to the news, filled me with dismay, as lies were being garbed to resemble truth, by the politicians and their spin doctors. This got me thinking and my thoughts then crystallised into this poem.

TRUTH AND LIES

This has been my recipe for happiness. I have always
maintained that the key to happiness, lies in managing one's
expectations. It is best to have no or low expectations. And
the best way to achieve it, is by letting go. If you don't cling to
things, then you will never get hurt.

LET IT GO

This poem is essentially my autobiography, in a nutshell.
Here I go back into my memories, and pick out snippets of
importance and relevance, to my journey through life. It
predominantly consists of the joys of my life, as my nature
is to think, that my glass is never half empty,
but always half full!

SUITCASE

Pulak Sahay

Written 10 days after the 18th Lok Sabha election results were declared, on the 4th of June, 2024. BJP was the largest party, with more seats on its own, than the entire opposition alliance put together. But still it did not get a clear majority on its own, contrary to the previous 2 elections. It did however form the government on the 9th of June with its pre poll allies, the NDA. So although the BJP with its partners, the NDA, has been victorious in forming the government, the victory seems like defeat, as it has not lived up to its expectations, of crossing the 400-seat mark, losing big time in UP, with the margin of winning votes for Modi Ji himself, dropping by 3 lakhs.

VICTORY'S DEFEAT

Rest of the poems were written on topics that were handed down by the host who was organising the poetry get-together. This happens in our Suniye-Sunaiye group every 2-3 moths, and we all take turns in playing the host.

OTHERS

Dr. Pulak Sahay is a thespian who has done a host of plays from Arthur Miller, Tennessee Williams, and Noel Coward to Robert Bolt and Shakespeare from his teenage years till he was in his mid-fifties. Soon after leaving the amateur stage, he switched to writing poetry which has culminated in a book of poems that he artistically has collated now, into what he calls *"A Bouquet of Poems"*.

Apart from poetry, Dr. Sahay paints in acrylic, and is a keen wildlife and landscape photographer, and is in the process of writing a book on medieval Indian history, with his grandchildren, as the target audience.

Dr. Pulak Sahay was a Consultant Gastroenterologist in the National Health Service (NHS) of UK, for nearly 30 years. Being the upper gut cancer lead in his Trust, he was so distraught by the lack of knowledge regarding "Reflux Disease" amongst his patients, that in April 2010 he launched a medical charity called CARD (Campaign Against Reflux Disease) which is a Registered UK charity, whose sole aim is to spread education about the banes and complications of Reflux Disease, as well as outline its life style management. The CARD charity website is **www.cardcharity.co.uk** where important information is available regarding Reflux Disease.

About the Author

Dr. Sahay did hold a One Man exhibition of his paintings and poetry at Pontefract in West Yorkshire, UK where he sold his work and donated the entire proceeds to a Reflux Disease charity.

Using his photographs he has made greeting cards, that he has sold with all proceeds going to the CARD Charity. He also has a photography website which is **www.wildcardcharity.com** and which was launched in July 2023 where wildlife and landscape photographs taken by him, from all the 7 continents over a period of 18 years are displayed. Everything that Dr. Pulak Sahay now does, is always in aid of the CARD Charity, with the aim of spreading medical education about Reflux Disease. To prevent and curb the onslaught of Reflux Disease, has now become his magnificent obsession.

The level of knowledge, regarding Reflux Disease which affects nearly 20% of the adult population in UK (11 million in absolute numbers) and 15% of adult population in India (112 million in absolute numbers) is woefully inadequate. As patients are unaware of the harm that can be caused by reflux, they don't seek medical advice. They consider reflux as part of normal modern life. This leads to poor quality of life and in the extreme situations can lead to oesophageal cancer, which is the fastest growing cancer in the West and is rising in India as well and has an appalling mortality.

To target this problem, CARD charity was launched by Dr. Pulak Sahay, Consultant Gastroenterologist in NHS, UK, on 23rd April 2010. Its sole aim is to educate the general masses, globally, regarding Reflux Disease. The website address is **www.cardcharity.co.uk** where information is available regarding Reflux Disease, its complications and its life style management.

Lords & Knights of the Realm of England along with a public celebrity are patrons of this charity.

Annual events have been organised to raise funds for CARD and calendars and greeting cards have been sold in aid of the CARD charity. The book of poetry called *"A Bouquet of Poems"* is being launched in 2024 and the proceeds from the sale will go to the CARD Charity and with the popularity of this book Dr. Sahay hopes that he will be able to bring Reflux disease centre stage.

About 
(Campaign Against Reflux Disease)

Campaign Against Reflux Disease

Divyangani Sharma is Art Director at IdeaWorks Design & Strategy Pvt. Ltd., a Delhi-NCR-based communication design, brand, and marketing strategy firm. From a young age, she has found solace and fascination in the world of art and design. What began as a mere pastime soon evolved into her safe haven, a source of completeness that transcended the boundaries of mere hobbyism. Today, art is not just her profession; it is the essence of her happiness, the euphoria of her existence. For her, art is more than just a medium of expression; it is an emotion, a language that transcends verbal communication. Through her creations, she articulates thoughts and feelings that language cannot express.

"A Bouquet of Poems" is a rich anthology capturing the profound reflections and emotional depth of the poet, Dr. Pulak Sahay. The collection spans a wide array of themes, each poem rooted in personal experiences and societal observations. From the contemplation of nature in "The Colour Green" to the heart-wrenching scenes of "India's Tragedy" and the jubilant celebration of family in "Eila Anamsa," Dr. Sahay's work reflects a journey through life's multifaceted experiences. The poems are interwoven with personal narratives, each capturing life's experiences and emotions, making this collection a compelling and introspective read. The emotive and compelling nature of the poems made it easy for Divyangani to reflect their emotions and themes in the design.

As a designer and artist, her goal for this book was to visually convey the emotions behind each poem through illustrations. She says that Dr. Sahay very graciously allowed her the freedom to explore her creativity while designing the book. While reading each poem, she aimed to understand the major emotions and symbolism and bring them to life. This illustrative poem book has come to be with a minimalist yet illustrative design approach, giving each poem its unique personality while maintaining a cohesive look and feel.

About the Designer and the Design

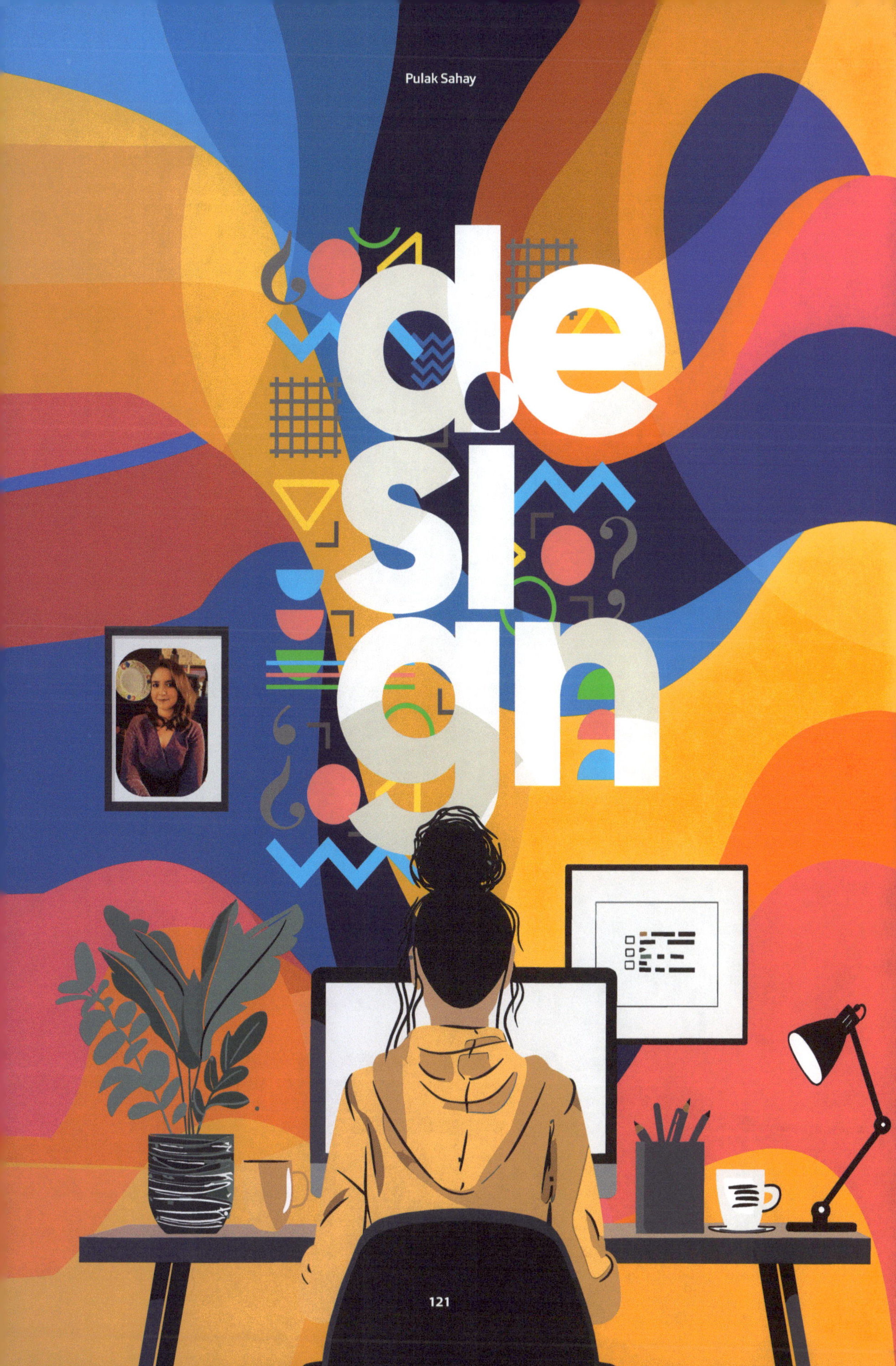

design